The Death of Hitler

The Death of Hitler

The Full Story with New Evidence from Secret Russian Archives

Ada Petrova and Peter Watson

W. W. NORTON & COMPANY
New York   London

W. W. Norton & Company, Inc.
500 Fifth Avenue, New York, NY 10110
W. W. Norton & Company Ltd.
10 Coptic Street, London WC1A 1PU

1 2 3 4 5 6 7 8 9 0

CONTENTS

LIST OF ILLUSTRATIONS

ACKNOWLEDGMENTS

We would like to thank the people in Moscow and in London who helped produce this book.

Above all, we thank Igor Torbakov, Russian historian and political analyst, for guidance and for acting as interpreter and translator of many documents. In Moscow we would also like to thank Konstantin Akinsha, Gregorii Kozlov and Mikhail Leschinsky for their advice and support.

Ada Petrova would also like to thank Professor Viktor Zyagin of the Federal Centre for Forensic Medical Examination, for his cooperation and scholarly expertise; and Anatoli Prokopenko, the former director of the Special Trophy Archive in Moscow. He gave Ada the first encouragement to research the Hitler archive.

In London, our thanks to Lord Bullock, who read the typescript, Bernard Clark, Kate Mosse, Alexander Archer, Emily Stillman and John Laurence for their support and technical help. Peter Watson would also like to thank Patricia and John Menzies for their generous hospitality during the writing of this book.

Any errors that remain in *The Death of Hitler* are, of course, ours and ours alone.

MAP OF THE BUNKER UNDER THE REICHSCHANCELLERY

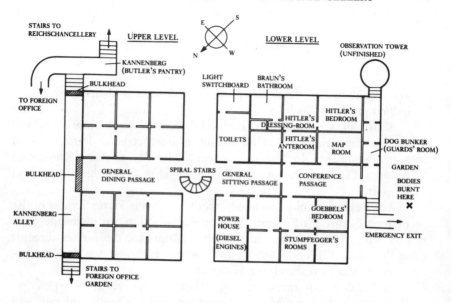

STAIRS TO
REICHSCHANCELLERY

UPPER LEVEL

E   S

N   W

LOWER LEVEL

OBSERVATION TOWER
(UNFINISHED)

KANNENBERG
(BUTLER'S PANTRY)

LIGHT
SWITCHBOARD

BRAUN'S
BATHROOM

BULKHEAD

TO FOREIGN
OFFICE

HITLER'S
BEDROOM

HITLER'S
DRESSING-ROOM

TOILETS

HITLER'S
ANTEROOM

MAP
ROOM

DOG BUNKER
(GUARDS' ROOM)

GARDEN

BULKHEAD

GENERAL
DINING PASSAGE

SPIRAL STAIRS

GENERAL
SITTING PASSAGE

CONFERENCE
PASSAGE

BODIES
BURNT
HERE

KANNENBERG
ALLEY

GOEBBELS'
BEDROOM

POWER
HOUSE

(DIESEL
ENGINES)

STUMPFEGGER'S
ROOMS

EMERGENCY EXIT

BULKHEAD

STAIRS TO
FOREIGN OFFICE
GARDEN

DIAGRAM OF THE SKULL

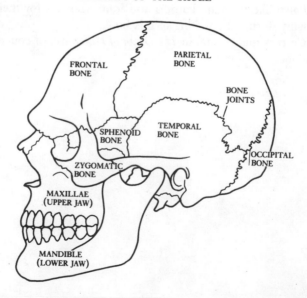

PARIETAL
BONE

FRONTAL
BONE

BONE
JOINTS

TEMPORAL
BONE

SPHENOID
BONE

OCCIPITAL
BONE

ZYGOMATIC
BONE

MAXILLAE
(UPPER JAW)

MANDIBLE
(LOWER JAW)

CHRONOLOGY OF THE
LAST DAYS IN THE BERLIN BUNKER

1945

January 16 Hitler returns to Berlin from Adlerhorst and enters the Bunker. "Hitler never saw another sunrise or sunset after 16 January."

February 25 Leaves the Bunker to address a secret meeting of Gauleiters outside Berlin. He returns the same day.

March 15 Leaves the Bunker at noon for the east front at Frankfurt on the Oder, about sixty miles away. He is away for four hours.

April 15 Eva Braun arrives, unbidden. She refuses to leave when Hitler asks her to do so.

April 16 Battle of Berlin begins and Operation Clausewitz conceived. This was the (ill thought-out) plan for the defence of the government quarter in Berlin.

April 20 Hitler's birthday. He is fifty-six. He adjourns to the Chancellery Court of Honour for the benefit of the newsreels. He is away from the Bunker for about an hour.
Himmler leaves the Bunker for the last time.

April 21 Professor Werner Haase arrives, to replace Theo Morrell and Ludwig Stumpfegger as Hitler's doctor.
Last American daylight raid on Berlin.
Dönitz leaves the Bunker for the last time.
The Steiner attack is ordered.

April 22 Morrell leaves the Bunker.
Steiner attack fails, letting the Russians inside the Berlin limits.

Hitler suffers nervous breakdown. Announces to his
staff that: "All is lost" and he will remain in Berlin
and commit suicide at the end.
Goebbels family arrive in the Bunker (each child with
one toy).
Operation Seraglio, the mass escape to
Berchtesgaden. Ten aircraft leave.
Goebbels broadcasts to the German nation that Hitler
is in Berlin and will stay there and fight with his
troops.

April 23   Göring sends telegram from Bavaria regarding the
succession.
Himmler meets Count Bernadotte (Swedish envoy in
Berlin) and briefs him about a surrender in the
West.

April 24   4 am: Speer leaves the Bunker for the last time.
Last overland roads out of Berlin are cut.

April 25   Russians capture Tempelhof airport and reach Berlin
inner ring, the Zitadelle.
Fegelein leaves the Bunker.

April 26   Ritter von Greim and Hanna Reitsch arrive in the
Bunker.

April 27   Fegelein's absence is noted; he is sought and brought
back to the Bunker.

April 28   Himmler's betrayal is discovered; Fegelein shot.
At midnight von Greim and Hanna Reitsch leave.

April 29   Just after midnight: Hitler marries Eva Braun.
2 am: Hitler writes his Will and Political Testament.
3.30: Bormann sends telegram to Dönitz: "The
Führer is alive and is conducting the defence of
Berlin . . ."
Josef and Magda Goebbels give a party for their
children in the afternoon.

April 30   4.30 am: Hitler retires.
5.30: Hitler rises.
Dönitz appointed his successor.

8.30 am: Hitler at breakfast when the Russian artillery stops.
10: Assault on the Reichstag begins.
Eva Braun seeks her last look at the sun.
1 pm: Lunch.
3: The final farewells, in the main corridor.
circa 3.15: Magda Goebbels breaks in to see Hitler. Axmann arrives in the Bunker. Günsche will not allow him to see the Führer.
circa 3.30: Death of Hitler and Eva Braun.
4-4.15: The bodies are burned.
10: Günsche sends a soldier to look at the bodies.

April 30- May 1	Around midnight: Rattenhuber orders the bodies to be buried in a nearby bomb crater.
May 1	Early: Krebs negotiates a ceasefire and crosses the lines to surrender. His conditions are refused and he returns to the Bunker. 2 pm: Three Goebbels children play in front of Misch. 5.30: All six Goebbels children given doped chocolate, then poison. 6: Death of Goebbels children. 8.30: Death of Josef and Magda Goebbels. 10.20: Dönitz broadcasts the news about Hitler's death, claiming the Führer had died that day fighting with his troops. 11: The break-out begins.
May 2	9 am: Twelve Russian women of the Russian Army Medical Corps stumble across the Bunker. The last man, Johannes Hentschel, gives himself up. Mid-morning: First Russian combat troops enter the Bunker. Just after noon, Klimenko arrives and finds body of Josef Goebbels.
May 3	Klimenko returns, finds bodies of Krebs and Goebbels children.
May 4	Klimenko finds corpses of Hitler and Braun in bomb crater but reburies them.

May 5	Klimenko learns that "double" is not Hitler. Returns to crater and exhumes corpses he had found the day before.
May 8	VE Day. Autopsies begin.

PREFACE

This book is a detective story. It explores one of the most enduring mysteries of our day: how, exactly, did Adolf Hitler die? For fifty years historians, soldiers, forensic doctors and weapons experts have wrangled over Hitler's last days, painstakingly piecing together the evidence in an effort to understand what happened in the Berlin Bunker in the last week of April 1945. New theories have appeared every few years, each one adding to the story – and to the mystery and confusion. No one yet has been able to answer all the doubts and uncertainties which remain since then.

This book began when its British author, Peter Watson, was in New York in January 1995 attending a conference entitled "The Spoils of War". This conference was a first attempt to bring together scholars from several countries – most notably Russia and Germany – to try to settle the issue of what to do about the many paintings and sculptures and other art objects that had been taken from Germany by the Red Army at the end of World War Two and which were now turning up in Russia. Peter Watson's previous book, a biography of the Russian dancer Rudolf Nureyev, had taken him to Russia many times. There he had befriended Konstantin Akinsha and Gregorii Kozlov, the two art historians and journalists who had first exposed the fact that the gold of Troy – known as Schliemann's Treasure – which was taken from Berlin at the end of World War Two, was actually in the basement of the Pushkin Museum in Moscow.

During the conference Akinsha and Kozlov had breakfast with Watson. For two reasons this proved to be an exciting encounter. In the first place, the restaurant was robbed during the meal. Shouting and fighting broke out as the thief made his getaway. All seasoned New Yorkers, mindful that Manhattan robbers are usually armed, dropped to the floor. Only Akinsha, Kozlov and Watson remained eating, sitting targets. Fortunately, this must have been the only time a New York robber did not carry a gun for he was soon overpowered and led away.

But the more enduring cause of excitement during the breakfast was Akinsha and Kozlov's comment that they had a friend in Moscow who was also a journalist who had a "world scoop". She wished to bring it out to the West. Could Watson help?

What was the scoop, he asked. "Peter," Akinsha said, "this woman is called Ada. She has found Hitler's skull."

In the summer of 1992, Ada Petrova approached Anatoli Prokopenko, director of the State Special Trophy Archive in Moscow. Ada is a well-known journalist in Russia and has won several awards for her television programmes. She was, for instance, the first journalist allowed to film in the "gulag", the Russian "archipelago" of camps and prisons which housed thousands – if not hundreds of thousands – political prisoners and exiles for decades under Stalin, Brehznev and Andropov. She was the journalist who located Victor Hamilton, an American who defected to the Soviet Union in the early 1960s. Far from finding a comfortable retirement in a government dacha, as Kim Philby or Guy Burgess had done, he had been held in a "psychiatric hospital" for nearly thirty years. For another television programme, Ada had discovered the fate of Raoul Wallenberg, the Swedish diplomat who disappeared in mysterious circumstances. She worked for five years covering the war in Afghanistan. She filmed Svetlana Stalin in London and had taken her story back to Russia. Ada Petrova had a good track record of programme making, she was not afraid of controversy and was no mouthpiece for the government.

In mid-1992, when Petrova went to visit Prokopenko, she was interested in making a programme on the death of Stalin. She was mystified by what exactly had gone on inside the Kremlin between Stalin's stroke at the end of February 1953 and his death in the first week of March. Naturally, her first port of call was the State Special Trophy Archive, which is now housed inside the Kremlin in the white and ochre building that used to be Stalin's old apartments. She wanted to see what documents there were that could throw light on this period. In the wake of Gorbachev's ascent to power and his subsequent replacement by Yeltsin, many archival materials in Russia were becoming more accessible. Ada hoped to take advantage of that fact.

It didn't quite work out like that. She and Prokopenko had several friends in common and they got on so well in their preliminary conversations that they decided to have dinner together in the canteen in the basement of the archives.

Ada and Prokopenko set off along the corridor of the archive towards the lift, when they happened to pass the open door of an office. Inside, a radio was playing. The music was "Chorus of the Hebrew Slaves," from Verdi's opera *Nabucco*. Casually, just making conversation, Ada remarked to Prokopenko: "Did you know that *Nabucco* was one of Hitler's favourite operas?" She thought it ironic, in view of the Führer's rabid anti-semitism, that he should be so fond of an opera with a chorus of Hebrew slaves.

Mumbling that he didn't know much about Hitler's tastes in opera, Prokopenko then added something that was to take Ada's mind off dinner – and Stalin – completely. "What I do know," he said, "is that I've got Hitler's skull right here in this archive."

In fact, Prokopenko had much more than just Hitler's skull. Ada discovered his uniforms, charred and tattered. She discovered forty-two unknown drawings and watercolours which show that Hitler was a somewhat better painter than he was often given credit for. She discovered his personal photograph album, displaying the Führer in some extraordinary poses. But most important of all, she found an entire archive devoted to Hitler and his death, six buff-coloured files together with albums with more photographs mounted on blue card. They show in detail what happened in Berlin in the last chaotic days.

Many historians have suspected that something like the Hitler archive had to exist in Russia. Here, at last, is the confirmation. But in this book we do more – we hope – than just present the new pieces of evidence contained in the Moscow file. We try to fit this fresh evidence into what has gone before, to explain how certain historians have been correct in their assumptions and conclusions all along, and how others have been wrong. As well as adding to the story – in a way, providing the final chapter to half a century of historical detective work – we provide as complete a guide as possible to the many different researches into Hitler's death.

For this is a story that spans fifty years and, for most of that time, the world was divided by the Iron Curtain. As the speculation and theories about Hitler's demise built up in the West, Soviet Russia maintained a complete silence. Only on two occasions did they release any information, and even then allowing publication of a version of events that was seriously incomplete.

In telling this story, we therefore take the reader right back to the beginning – Berlin 1945 – when Hitler's whereabouts were still a mystery to the Allied Forces. We then move forward, following along the trail of others, until we reach the present – Moscow 1995 – and our own findings. Those who are already familiar with other books on the death of Hitler may wish to concentrate on Chapters 5, 6 and 7, where the new material is introduced and discussed in depth. For others who are unfamiliar with this older material we hope that our summary will convey the truly exciting way this detective story has evolved over the years.

This is an historical tale that has been mystified, obfuscated and covered up for two generations. At last, we dare to suggest, the whole truth may be told.

London & Moscow, April 1995

Part I

Hitler's Body

1

THE LAST PRIZE

On a cold afternoon at the end of March 1945, General Dwight D. Eisenhower sat down at his headquarters in Reims, north-eastern France and drafted an unprecedented and historic cable. It was sent to Moscow, for the personal attention of Joseph Stalin. This was the first time in all the years of war that the Supreme Commander of the Allied Expeditionary Force had communicated directly with the Soviet leader, but there were now urgent and pressing reasons for doing so. The final thrust of the Allied Forces deep into Germany was about to begin and it was clearly important for the Anglo-American armies to coordinate their movements with the Russians. Eisenhower told Stalin his plans and asked that he reciprocate, wanting to avoid a repeat of the situation in 1939. Then, in a very different phase of hostilities, German and Russian troops – allied by treaty – had met head-on in Poland when that country was being carved up between Stalin and Hitler. No pre-arranged line of demarcation had been fixed, which had resulted in a battle with surprisingly heavy casualties on both sides. In the climate of suspicion that was developing between America and Britain on the one hand, and Russia on the other, such a clash had to be avoided at all costs. It could bring catastrophe at this vital stage of the War.

Eisenhower sent two other cables that afternoon, one to Washington, to the General of the Army, George C. Marshall, who was his immediate superior. The other went to General Bernard Montgomery, Commander-in-Chief of the 21st Army Group in the north of Germany. To both men, Eisenhower outlined his new plan for bringing a speedy end to the War. It centred on the 12th Army Group, under General Omar N. Bradley, which would advance through central Germany on the Erfurt-Leipzig-Dresden axis. There, Eisenhower hoped, it would join hands with the Russians and divide Germany in two.

Within hours, those telegrams – especially the one to Stalin – had created the most serious split between the Americans and the British since the invasion had begun nine months earlier on D Day, 6 June 1944. For the fact was, in the days and weeks prior to 28 March, Eisenhower had changed his mind decisively on one vital matter relating to the course of the war: he no longer considered Berlin, capital of Hitler's Reich, to be a major military objective. Unlike British generals, Eisenhower had not been trained to consider political objectives as part of military strategy. His main concern was to get the War over as quickly as possible and with as few casualties as circumstances would allow. In international terms, Eisenhower was politically inexperienced. His mission, as spelled out by the Combined Chiefs of Staff, was enshrined in one sentence: "You will enter the continent of Europe and, in conjunction with the other United Nations, undertake operations aimed at the heart of Germany and the destruction of her armed forces." Even now, this late in the war, his objective was purely military – to destroy the enemy army as quickly as he could. In any case, it had already been agreed at higher levels that Berlin would fall under Soviet aegis.

For the British in general – and Prime Minister Winston Churchill in particular – the shape of the post-War world was already clear. Like Czechoslovakia and Poland, much of Eastern Europe was already under the Russian heel, destined for Communist rule. If Montgomery could capture Berlin ahead of the Russians it would be a major propoganda victory and give the Western Allies an important bargaining advantage later on. For Churchill had already noted with misgiving the changes in Stalin's behaviour since the conference between him, Stalin and Roosevelt at Yalta in February 1945, where the map of the post-1945 world had been sketched in. For example, Anglo-American bombers forced to land behind Russian lines were now being interned, along with their crews; the Russians had refused the evacuation of Anglo-American soldiers in eastern camps, although reciprocal arrangements were going ahead for Russian soldiers in western camps; air bases and refuelling and repair facilities for American bombers on Russian-controlled territory were being denied. In these proto-Cold War circumstances, Churchill considered Eisenhower's telegram to Stalin a naïve and dangerous intervention into global political strategy. He was incensed.

There were, however, several reasons (good and bad) for Eisenhower's change of heart over Berlin. He heartily disliked Montgomery, who was in command in the north. To have settled on a dash for Berlin would have given the British Field-Marshal a bigger role than Eisenhower could have stomached. But it is another reason which particularly concerns us here. At this stage of the War, the Supreme Headquarters of the Allied Expeditionary Force (SHAEF), were located in the three-storey Collège Moderne et Technique in a back street of Reims, close to the railway station. There, near Eisenhower's own office, was the map room. On the wall there hung a chart that was updated every day. Headed *Reported National Redoubt*, it showed the mountainous, lakeland region south of Munich, stretching over into western Austria. This incorporated Bavaria and OberSalzburg, the very region where the Nazi Party had been born a quarter of a century before. It was an area some 20,000 square miles in dimension, consisting mainly of wooded mountain peaks between 7000 and 9000 feet high. At its heart was Berchtesgaden and Hitler's mountain-top hideaway, the "Eagle's Nest".

The National Redoubt map was covered in red marks, each one a military symbol denoting this or that defence installation. A Y meant a radio transmitter, a square stood for barracks, a crescent with an F inside indicated a food dump. There were signs for ammunition stores, for petrol and chemical warfare dumps and for underground factories. Fortified positions were shown with zig-zag lines. Every day during March more symbols were added to the chart, so much so that this mountain defence system, the National Redoubt, seemed to SHAEF the greatest remaining threat in the European war, greater even than the prize of Berlin.

It was in this Alpine area, according to Allied Intelligence, that the Nazis intended to make their last stand, with Adolf Hitler at their head. The terrain was so difficult as to be almost impregnable but, again according to intelligence, the remaining Nazi leadership would not be content merely to sit back and absorb whatever the Allies could throw at them. A new type of commando unit had been created, called the Were-wolves, whose task it was to sneak out from the Redoubt and create mayhem among the occupation armies. Some 200,000 veteran troops and Werewolves were to cover an area of 20,000 square miles, it was rumoured, to Bavaria, Austria and a small part of Italy.

Some plans certainly went ahead. Both Otto Skorzeny and Reinhard Gehlen hid plans and microfilms in the Alpine Fortress area, Gehlen claiming to have based his organisation on his secret intelligence on Polish resistance to the Nazis. Gehlen had documents forged on his behalf and transferred his wife and children to the Alps. William Casey, an Allied Intelligence officer, later recalled being told in early May 1945 that the Werewolf organisation was in process of formation and that it was to be built on the framework of the Gestapo and other Nazi security services.

The Allies' concern with the Redoubt and Hitler's last stand had been growing since September 1944 when the OSS had predicted that, as the War neared its end, the Nazis would evacuate crucial government departments to Bavaria. The War Department in Washington had taken up this notion on 12 February 1945, warning that a man like Hitler would require his *Götterdämmerung*. Four days later, Allied agents in Switzerland sent a chilling report claiming that the Nazis were preparing for "a bitter fight from the mountain redoubt". This report said that strongpoints within the Alpine Fortress were connected by underground railways, that months of supply of munitions had been gathered together with "almost all of Germany's poison gas supplies."

Not everyone was convinced. The Research and Analysis Branch of OSS, directed by Bill Langer, produced a mammoth report: "An analysis of the political and social organisation, the communications, economic controls, agricultural and food supply, mineral resources, manufacturing and transportation facilities of south Germany". It was very sceptical of the viability of a National Redoubt but, as its very title implied, the report was too long, too dry and too academic-sounding to be read by busy field officers. No one paid it the attention it deserved.

Instead, on 21 March, the headquarters staff of General Bradley's 12th Army Group released what turned out to be a decisive memorandum – "Re-Orientation of Strategy" – which argued that Allied objectives had changed rendering "obsolete the plans which brought us over the beaches." The strategy document concluded that the significance of Berlin was now much diminished and that: "all indications suggest that the enemy's political and military directorate is already in the process of displacing to the Redoubt in lower Bavaria."

Four days after that came the most alarming analysis of all. The Chief of Intelligence of Lieutenant-General Alexander Patch's 7th Army, on the southern edge of the front, described an élite force of mainly SS and mountain troops, at least 200,000 to 300,000 strong. The report said that up to five very long trains were arriving in the Redoubt area every week and that new types of weapon had been observed on these trains. An underground factory was believed to exist in the Alpine Fortress capable of producing Messerschmitts. Werewolf schools were reported everywhere and Counter-Intelligence Corps estimates put the numbers of youngsters in training under SS officers at some 5000 in one particular week. A booklet had been published that, "reinforced a general sense of apprehension". It was entitled *Werewolf: Winke für Jagdeinheiten* (Tips for Hunting Units). The *Vogelfrei* legends were revived.

"The word meant 'bird-free', explained the report. It derived from the mediaeval-style courts of revenge, which declared that anyone found guilty became like a game bird during the open season for hunters."

Goebbels chipped in. His broadcasts – and those of Radio Werewolf – stepped up the pressure. "God has given up the protection of the people ... Satan has taken command." Goebbels himself said, "We Werewolves consider it our supreme duty to kill, to kill and to kill, employing every cunning and wile in the darkness of the night, crawling, groping through towns and villages, like wolves, noiselessly, mysteriously." There were secret recognition signals for boys and girls (some were only nine) and the *Wolfsangel*, a runic letter, was to be painted on buildings occupied by those marked out for vengeance.

Then there was the rumour about Gallery 16, near the village of Redl Zipf, part of the Alpine Fortress. This gallery was an underground network of corridors and workshops centred around a 200 foot tunnel into which banknote presses had been transferred from Berlin. Nine million Bank of England notes with a face value of $600 million were produced here, sufficient for the Bank to have to withdraw many of its own notes and substitute a new design with a fine metallic thread drawn through the fabric in a way thought to be immune to forgery.

In March, SHAEF itself finally and crucially concluded that: "It seems reasonably certain that some of the most important ministries and personalities of the Nazi regime are already established in the Redoubt area. Göring, Himmler, Hitler are said to be in the process of withdrawing to their respective personal mountain strongholds." Even those who had their reservations, such as SHAEF's Intelligence Chief, the British Major-General Kenneth Strong, thought that the Allies should act *as though* the Redoubt existed, just in case. We repeat that there were other reasons for Eisenhower's change of mind over Berlin. We have dwelt on this one because the Redoubt idea produced in the mind-set of the Allied Command the sense that if – and when – Hitler was found it would be in the south.

The Allies in fact found out the grim truth on 23 April when three Germans crossed the Elbe near Magdeburg shortly after dawn and surrendered to the US 30th Infantry Division. One of them was Lieutenant-General Kurt Dittmar, a fifty-seven-year-old Wehrmacht officer who had made a name for himself broadcasting communiqués from the front and was known everywhere as the "voice of the German High Command". As such he was considered the most accurate of the German military broadcasters and so drew a following not only in Germany but among the Allied monitoring staff.

Dittmar was immediately taken to headquarters for interrogation: "Tell us about the National Redoubt," someone demanded. Cornelius Ryan – author of the 1966 book *The Last Battle* – takes up the story: "Dittmar looked puzzled. The only thing he knew about a National Redoubt, he said, was something he had read in a Swiss newspaper the previous January. He agreed that there were pockets of resistance in the north, 'including Norway and Denmark and one in the south in the Italian Alps. But,' he added, 'that is less by intention than by force of circumstance.' As his interrogators pressed him about the redoubt, Dittmar shook his head. 'The National Redoubt? It's a romantic dream. It's a myth.'"

He was right.

General Bradley, whose general staff had written the famous memorandum on a change of strategy – in which the importance of Berlin was downgraded in favour of the Alpine Fortress – later had the grace to admit his error. "The Redoubt existed largely in the imagination of a few fanatical Nazis. It grew into so exaggerated a scheme that I am astonished we could have believed it as innocently as we did. But while it persisted, this legend . . . shaped our tactical thinking."

Dittmar had another surprise for his interrogators. Hitler, he said confidently, was in Berlin. Until that point no one on the Allied side had been exactly certain where the Führer was. His whereabouts and all personal details about him, such as his medical records, had been kept a well-guarded secret throughout the War. But while the Redoubt idea had dominated Allied minds it had been assumed that Hitler would be found there. One of the Allies' spies in Berlin, Carl Wiberg, a Swedish businessman generally regarded as a "good Berliner" by his neighbours, had sent a report on 18 April obtained from two women gossiping in a black market shop, to the effect that Hitler was in the Berlin area. But his report had been lost amid the weight of intelligence in the past five days. When the Allied interrogators suggested to Dittmar that he was mistaken, or dissembling, he refused to change his story. Moreover, he said, "Hitler will either be killed there or commit suicide."

It was thus against this background that the War entered its last month. Too late, the Allies realised that there was no National Redoubt in Bavaria, and never had been. (As late as 28 April, the *Daily Mirror* was able to report that "Seven Allied armies are closing in on Hitler's last-stand Redoubt in the mountains of Austria and Bavaria.") Too late they realised that Hitler and Stalin, whose lives had run in parallel for so long, both believed that Berlin itself was the last great prize, both psychologically and politically.

For our story, the most important consequence of this course of events was that the Russians reached Berlin first. Indeed, the moment Stalin received Eisenhower's cable which suggested that Berlin was no longer very important, he ordered Marshal Zhukov to advance on the German capital with all speed and whatever the cost. He couldn't believe that Eisenhower could be so wrong, or so naïve – and therefore assumed that he must be playing a political game. Churchill had been right to be annoyed about the "historic and unprecedented" telegram.

The Anglo-American forces, following Eisenhower's new policy, actually met the Russian Army along the Elbe, first coming into contact at Torgau on 25 April. Running north, at its closest point this "Front Line" was just under fifty miles from Berlin. It wasn't much but it was enough.

It was not until the conference of Commanders-in-Chief of the four armies of occupation on 29 June, that the various Berlin zones were agreed upon. Advanced detachments of American, British and French troops arrived in the city at the beginning of July. Thus the Russians had had Berlin – and the Reichschancellery – all to themselves for about seven weeks, for most of May and all of June. This, and the developing Cold War, accounted for much of what followed.

On 1 May, at 9.30 in the evening, Hamburg radio warned the German people that "a grave and important announcement" was about to be made. This was immediately followed by several excerpts from a number of Wagner's operas and the slow movement of Bruckner's Seventh Symphony. Then at 10.20 pm, came the voice of Grand-Admiral Karl Dönitz, Commander-in-Chief for the north of Germany. In sombre tones, he announced the death of Hitler and his own succession as Führer of the Reich. Hitler had fallen "this afternoon," he said, fighting "at the head of his troops".

This statement was believed by many. *The Times* of London printed Hitler's obituary next day. President Valera of Ireland sent his condolences to the German ambassador in Dublin. But it was untrue. Hitler, as the world was later told, had died the previous day and had not fallen in action, as a heroic martyr, but had committed suicide without leaving the Bunker under the Reichschancellery where he had been since 16 January 1945. Dönitz perhaps had more than one reason for releasing the story he did. He may not have been aware of all the facts, but in any case he must have wondered how the German troops would have reacted if they had been told that their leader had not died a glorious death but had taken his own life.

Whatever Dönitz's reasons, this erroneous story, combined with the complete silence on the part of the Russians regarding what they had or had not found in the Reichschancellery and the absence of a body – either Hitler's or Eva Braun's – did not convince many people. On the contrary, throughout the summer of 1945 the rumours that Hitler was still alive gathered pace.

There were many sightings. Among the first, it was reported that Hitler had been seen living as a hermit in a cave near Lake Garda in northern Italy. Another report had it that he was now a shepherd in the Swiss Alps, a third that he was a croupier at a casino in Evian. He was seen at Grenoble, St Gallen and even off the Irish coast.

Viewed from this distance, each of these accounts appears fantastic and incredible. But that was not how they were seen at the time. Not all of the accounts were so fantastic. In July 1945, the US Office of Censorship intercepted a letter written from someone in Washington. Addressed to a Chicago newspaper, the letter claimed that Hitler was living in a German-owned hacienda 450 miles from Buenos Aires. The US government gave this report enough credibility to act on it, sending a classified telegram to the American embassy in Argentina requesting help in following up the inquiry. Besides giving basic information the telegram added that Hitler was alleged to be living in special underground quarters. "Source indicates that there is a western entrance to the underground hideout which consists of a stone wall operated by photo-electric cells, activated by code signals from ordinary flashlights. Entrance thus uncovered supposedly provides admittance for automobiles." It continued that Hitler had provided himself with two doubles and was hard at work developing plans for the manufacture of long-range robot bombs and other weapons. The matter was taken sufficiently seriously for J. Edgar Hoover, then the director of the FBI, to become involved, although shortly afterwards he wrote to the War Department: "To date, no serious indication has been received that Adolf Hitler is in Argentina."

The Russian newspaper *Izvestiia* ran a report that Hitler and Eva Braun were both alive and well, and living in a moated castle in Westphalia. This implied complicity on the part of the British, for Westphalia lay in the British zone of occupation. The report was followed by one in August, in which an American lawyer wrote to Hoover at the FBI to say that the former Führer was living under the alias of Gerhardt Weithaupt in a house belonging to a certain Frau Frieda Haaf at Innsbruck. With Hitler, said this lawyer, was his personal physician, Dr Alfred Jodl.

Another account also placed Hitler at Innsbruck. The informant was an educated man – again a lawyer – rather than a peasant or an ill-educated private soldier. Another came from a German doctor, a man presumably trained in observation. Karl-Heinz Spaeth claimed he had treated Hitler on 1 May 1945 at his Berlin casualty clearing station in the cellar of the Landwehrkasino right opposite the Bunker at the Berlin Zoo. Spaeth said that Hitler had been wounded at a tank barricade in the fighting around the Küstrin area of the city. In his sworn deposition, he added: "Hitler was lowered to the floor. A shell fragment had pierced the uniform, went through his chest and entered the lungs on both sides. It was no use to do anything. I took a few first-aid bandages and bandaged him. During this time Hitler groaned continually. He was not fully conscious. To relieve his pain I went back to the collecting station to get some morphine and gave him a double strength injection. The general opinion was that Hitler would die. I examined his pulse and respiration and found that after about three minutes he had stopped breathing. The heartbeats continued for about three minutes and then ceased. After I had pronounced the Führer dead and had informed the SS leaders of this fact I was released and went back to my work." Shortly afterwards, Spaeth said, the surviving SS leaders "blew the body into the air with two three-kilo charges of high explosives." He repeated his story to an officer of the Military Government, who in turn reported to Berlin in September. Everyone, everywhere, seemed determined to ignore Grand-Admiral Dönitz's statement of 1 May.

Such accounts of Hitler's death were scarcely less confusing than the more numerous examples of sightings and the situation looked like getting out of hand. General George C. Marshall, the American Chief of Staff, had realised as early as 1 May that it might be necessary to do something to counter the "Hitler martyr myth" which had been fuelled by Admiral Dönitz's announcement. Eisenhower seemed not to agree. In June, when he was probably the most popular leader in the West, he attended a press conference at the Hotel Raphael in Paris. There he voiced doubt that Hitler was really dead. He was the first Allied figure of authority in the West to say this.

Nonetheless it was not until September that any official inquiry got under way – and when it did it was the British who carried out the investigations. Dick White, the Brigadier commanding the Intelligence Bureau in the British Zone of Occupation (part of MI5), was stationed at Bad Oeynhausen, between Osnabruck and Hannover, and he had been incensed by the Russian report that Adolf Hitler and Eva Braun were living, apparently unmolested, in the British zone of Germany – ie, Westphalia. He invited a young major, and friend, Hugh Trevor-Roper, to make an official inquiry into the mystery which at that time still surrounded the death of Hitler.

A four-volume dossier on the Führer, compiled by the US Counter-Intelligence Corps, was made available to Trevor-Roper who, in civilian life, was an Oxford history don. This dossier was "a cornucopia of everything that could be gleaned about" Hitler and included his medical condition, his state of mind, his various "inclinations and proclivities." It did *not* make Hitler out to be a monster. The CIC analysts had found, "to their embarrassment, that the scourge of the human race gave presents to children, hated blood sports, disliked excessively fanatical people and was conservative and fastidious in his habits ... Every day at the same hour," according to one informant, "he would go with the same dog to the same corner of the same field and pick up the same piece of wood and throw it in the same direction." The report also contained the conclusions of a long-distance psychiatric examination of the Führer. This concluded that the suicide of Hitler could not be ruled out.

Trevor-Roper's inquiries were to prove exciting. He spent most of September and October tracking down what eye-witnesses he could, people who had lived in the Führerbunker in those last desperate days and could tell him what had happened. He was not entirely successful. Goebbels and Martin Bormann were not available, missing or dead according to whom you talked to. So were Heinz Linge, Hitler's valet, Otto Günsche, Hitler's Adjutant, Hans Baur, his personal pilot and Johann Rattenhuber, the Chief of Bodyguards. Many others known to have been in the Bunker were also untraceable.

Still, Trevor-Roper was able to interview Frau Gerda Christian and Frau Else Krueger, who were respectively Hitler's and Bormann's secretaries. They had not actually been eye-witnesses for much of what happened, but they had been given contemporaneous accounts by people such as Linge and Günsche, who claimed to have seen everything. Trevor-Roper had also visited Innsbruck, no doubt to double-check the story that Hitler was now masquerading as Gerhardt Weithaupt.

On 1 November 1945, Trevor-Roper gave a press conference in Berlin where he outlined the conclusions of his inquiry. His investigations showed, he said, that Hitler had committed suicide at about 3.30 pm on 30 April 1945, and that Eva Braun had died with him. In Hitler's case, the manner of death was by shooting – the Führer had put a pistol in his mouth and pulled the trigger. In the case of Eva Braun, she had taken a cyanide capsule: everyone living in the Bunker had been issued with similar capsules.

Asked by one of the newspapermen if he was aware of the Russian view on Hitler's death, Trevor-Roper indicated that he thought the Soviets were sceptical – that is, inclined to the view that Hitler was *not* dead. As he said this, a Russian officer present nodded.

Trevor-Roper also dismissed the possibility that it was Hitler's doppelgänger – his double – who had been burned. In the first place, he said, there wouldn't have been time to move the double's body in and out of the Bunker. Second, in his very poor physical condition, Hitler would not have been able to escape. And third, and most convincingly perhaps, Eva Braun herself would never have died willingly – or been taken in by – such a substitute.

Finally, he conceded that there was no "conclusive proof" that Martin Bormann, Hitler's Personal – and Party – Secretary, was dead.

Although it was acknowledged that Trevor-Roper's account was necessarily incomplete and that there were many gaps to be filled in, the press conference was reported extensively in the world's newspapers. He himself continued to inquire into the last days of the Third Reich throughout the winter of 1945-46.

Later in the year, the Allied Intelligence services received word that a certain Paustin, working as a gardener in the quiet village of Tegernsee, was in fact none other than the former SS Standartenführer Wilhelm Zander, the Adjutant to Martin Bormann. Now here was a very important individual indeed. For three weeks in November and December 1945, British secret service agents and American CIC special agents Arnold Weiss and Rosener tried to track Paustin/Zander's trail.

As Christmas arrived, they thought they had him cornered. On Boxing Day, Trevor-Roper and the CIC agents raided the house they had been watching, only to find that Zander had left the area to visit his fiancée who lived near Passau. Two days later, they were tipped off that a suitcase belonging to Zander could be found in the home of a certain Frau Irmgard Unterholzener in Tegernsee. They wasted no time in paying Frau Unterholzener a visit and picked up the suitcase. The case was searched thoroughly but initially proved of little interest. However, a secret compartment was then found inside which were several documents that had been brought out of the Bunker only forty-eight hours before Berlin fell. These documents were of the utmost historical importance.

Here was Hitler's Will and Political Testament. This confirmed what Trevor-Roper had been told about the last days in the Bunker. There was also Goebbels's Appendix to Hitler's Political Testament – further corroborative evidence that the picture Trevor-Roper was building up was essentially correct. Third, and perhaps most intriguing of all, there was the marriage contract of Adolf Hitler and Eva Braun. Trevor-Roper had been told by several of the people who had lived in the Führerbunker that Eva Braun had finally achieved her long-time aim to become the wife of the Führer. If Trevor-Roper had ever had any doubts about what he had been told, here was documentary support.

But the marriage contract was more than just corroborative evidence. The fact of Hitler's marriage tended to confirm the psychological portrait Trevor-Roper was putting together. Hitler had never felt the need to marry Braun before. Why should he do so in the last week of April 1945? The answer seemed clear: only if he was contemplating something dramatic.

To be double sure of the veracity of the documents, they turned them over to Major Anthony W. Lobb, Chief of the 3rd us Army CIC, who handed them on to the Assistant Chief of Staff, G-2. He, in turn, shipped them across the Atlantic to the United States. In Washington, an FBI forensic analysis of the paper and ink confirmed their authenticity.

Still in Germany, Trevor-Roper and CIC agent Arnold Weiss had followed Zander to the small village of Vilshofen, near the Czech border. There, Zander resisted arrest and a short gunfight ensued before he was overpowered. He was transferred to Munich and interrogated. He resisted for about ten hours but finally broke, revealing to Trevor-Roper many details of the last days in the Bunker which the former historian had gleaned from other, less well-placed sources.

This was early in 1946. Although everything Trevor-Roper was turning up now confirmed his initial conclusions about Hitler's last days, yet much of the rest of the world was still not convinced. Sightings of Hitler continued.

That year he was seen in Spain, where he was reported at the end of September as leading a wolf-pack of u-boats. For added verisimilitude, he was said to be suffering badly from seasickness. Next, he was reported as living on a farm at La Falda in Argentina although his appearance had been changed, according to this report, by a plastic surgeon who had performed the operation on the boat that ferried the Führer across the Atlantic from Europe to the new world.

Just before Christmas 1946 the US embassy in Stockholm received an anonymous letter addressed to the "Chief of the American Zone". Given that even Kurt Dittmar had admitted that there was a small redoubt in northern Scandinavia, this report was treated more seriously than many others. It read in part:

"If you look in the Bauerska mountains you will find a long cave about 466 metres or maybe even longer, with about ninety-two doors, well camouflaged. Hitler has here a room thirty by thirty metres, with electrical stoves, one big, one small. There is food there, cans of all kinds for several years ahead and lots of money of all kinds of currencies. There is also a pipe from the top of the mountain in which food can be dropped down. Those who bring food there are called 'Ravens'. Those who built this in the mountains have been killed long ago so it would not be discovered. When you have found it, I demand one sixth of what there is there and a jeep and a tractor. You will know my name when you have found him." On the reverse was written: "They had stolen horses and cows, hay and so on. They have plenty of ammunition and guns. A Swede who has a sixth sense is with them. He tells them all. Find these gentlemen. What will be done will be done soon."

Still another report in 1946 placed Hitler in Holland, in a coffee room in Amsterdam. This time the writer commented on the Führer's strange appearance – he had a very long body and long arms – but the informant also said that this Hitler still had direct links with the Gestapo and was trying to kill the writer, who therefore begged the Allied authorities to act quickly.

Another report placed Hitler in Zurich, saying he had aged dreadfully, that his hair had turned white, his body was bent forward and he took very short steps. He apparently had some form of lung infection for he coughed persistently. He preferred dark suits and hats and his demeanour was "similar to that of a pensioned official." The Deputy Director of Intelligence at the European Command instructed his subordinates to check out this report, as he did with almost all such paperwork coming across his desk. "I feel we would be remiss in our duty," he wrote, "if we failed to follow up a report of this nature." He even requested help from the Chief of the Swiss Federal Police in Berne.

Nor were the Allied Forces immune from spotting Hitler. One

American GI reported that he had seen the Führer, Eva Braun and her sister Gretl in Bernheim in the house where he collected his laundry. This man had to be Hitler, the GI felt, because he flew into a rage whenever the v-1 weapon was mentioned and "exhibited great sentiment over the photograph of a dog" which seems to have closely resembled Blondi, the Führer's own Alsatian.

The impact of these reports may be judged from the account of Lieutenant Colonel W. Byford-Jones, a British Intelligence officer who, on 20 April 1946 (what would have been Hitler's fifty-seventh birthday), questioned twenty educated Berliners on the fate of Hitler. "Only one thought Hitler was dead. The other nineteen betrayed that they were conscious of the fact that it was their Führer's birthday. They were convinced he was alive and spoke of him with anything but reproach. I found also that children, who are usually a good guide to the beliefs of adults, almost without exception spoke of *Onkel Adolf* as a living being.

"A new feature in this belief was where Hitler was supposed to be hiding. In the summer of 1945 I had been told he was in Spain, South America and other unlikely places, but now another hide-out was mentioned. He was with the *Edelweiss*, an illegal organisation well known to exist, and he was in the wild mountainous area that extends from the Alps on the Swiss frontier to the Tyrol in Austria, where thousands of Wehrmacht troops, calling themselves *Edelweiss*, retain their wartime formations, stores, equipment and munitions and live high up in the mountain fastnesses." The Redoubt was back.

In January 1947, a report was sent to the American CIC forces via the French Intelligence services. This claimed that Hitler was hiding in the area of Heidelberg and was in touch with a Resistance leader in Weinheim. The French report said that Hitler had visited Weinheim disguised as an American soldier, the visit no doubt part of the Führer's campaign to begin a new Reich.

Weinheim duly became the subject of a raid by thirty Allied officers – five CIC special agents and twenty-five men of the US Constabulary. There was no trace of either Hitler or the Resistance leader.

It was in March 1947 that Trevor-Roper's report was published in the form of a book, under the title *The Last Days of Hitler*. By rights, the book ought to have solved the mystery once and for all, to have killed speculation for ever. It was meticulously researched, well written and by and large convincing. But among several points left unresolved, one all-important matter remained a mystery.

2

1945: "THESE BONES HAVE
NEVER BEEN FOUND"

The thrust of Hugh Trevor-Roper's findings regarding the death of Hitler – over seven editions of his book since 1947 – are too well known to be more than summarised here. But a brief resumé is needed, because it makes it clear just how much the Allies were kept in the dark by the Russians. It also helps explain why only now, fifty years after the end of the War, the full truth can at last be told.

Trevor-Roper began his account by discussing Hitler and the men and women around him, his court. Some of them were very powerful in the Reich and some of them were not, but they all shared the last days in the Bunker. The Bunker was a large suite of rooms built on two levels fifty feet beneath the gardens of the Reichschancellery in the centre of Berlin (see page viii). Next, Trevor-Roper then went on to discuss Hitler's behaviour and character in defeat, how his habits changed, how he became a neurotic recluse. He described the drugs prescribed for the Führer by Dr Theodor Morell and how all of Morell's medical rivals were dismissed, leaving the charlatan quack a free rein. Next he described the effect of impending defeat on Hitler's court, how Albert Speer – a former building manager, architect of the Reichschancellery itself and now Minister for Armaments – and Goebbels behaved; what Himmler did; how Eva Braun rallied to the Führer even as the others were looking out for themselves.

For our purposes, however, we may take up the story from the day of Hitler's fifty-sixth birthday, 20 April 1945. It is from that day that the final crucial changes began to overtake the man who had brought such mayhem on the world.

No one outside the Bunker – friend or enemy – was aware quite how strained the Führer was, both physically and mentally. Outwardly, all was well. That day, Joseph Goebbels – Hitler's Propaganda Minister – broadcast a birthday tribute, calling upon the German people to trust blindly in their leader and the stars: together, they would lead the nation to salvation. Inside the Bunker, however, all was far from well. Hitler's deteriorating health was a severe problem. For some time now, German newsreels had shown the Führer only from certain angles, on Goebbels' orders, so as not to damage the Hitler myth. It would have been easy to have done such damage, for in reality he was close to being a physical wreck. "Hitler's eyes, once iceberg blue and lustrous, were now often glazed," wrote Trevor-Roper, "the eyeballs sunken and bloodshot. His brown hair had turned suddenly grey. He no longer stood erect. His walk was bowed his body bent forward, and he often seemed in danger of losing his balance. Both hands trembled, and he used the right hand to hold the left up close to his body. While standing, he often leaned his left leg against a table for support. When he lay down on his couch, his senior valet, Linge, had to lift his feet from the floor to the couch. In the very last days, there was often spittle on his lips, and at times he simply drooled or whistled through his teeth. His complexion was sallow. Soup-slop and mustard spots now stained his once natty and spotless uniform jacket."

One of Hitler's security guards, Peter Hartmann, later said that on the day the Führer celebrated his birthday in 1945: "He seemed closer to seventy than fifty-six. He looked what I would call physically *senile*."

And it was another symptom of the extreme pressure that Hitler was under that he had recently changed his plans. By rights, on 20 April he ought to have been leaving Berlin for OberSalzberg where, in the "fabulous mountain cave of Barbarossa," he was to direct the battles for the south. Indeed, ten days before he had sent some servants south to prepare the house for his arrival.

But in those ten days one disaster had followed another. Trevor-Roper quotes Schwerin von Krosigk, the minister who kept a diary of the last days: "All through the week, there was nothing but a succession of Job's messengers." The Americans had crossed the Elbe in places and the Russians were threatening Dresden and Berlin, nearly cutting Germany in two. The British were on the outskirts of Bremen and Hamburg in the north and, in the south, the French had reached the upper Danube. The Russians were in Vienna and Patton was pushing through Bavaria. It was no better in Italy where Alexander had captured Bologna and had the wide, flat plains of the Po valley before him.

On his birthday, Hitler held a military conference and received a number of visitors. At one time or another, Göring, Goebbels, Himmler, General Alfred Jodl, Bormann, Field-Marshall Wilhelm Keitel,

Dönitz, Speer and his then Foreign Minister, Joachim von Ribbentrop, were each in attendance. The conference was bleak. Germany was within days, and maybe hours, of being divided and the Russians were in the process of encircling Berlin. Nazi policy at this time was for the armed forces to fall under two commands if the country was split – and Dönitz was told he would be in charge in the north. But Hitler couldn't make up his mind about the south and most of the other senior men in the Bunker urged him to leave Berlin, which they thought was doomed.

But he wouldn't go. He was racked with indecision, one sign of the nervous breakdown that was about to engulf him. Two people who did leave were Speer and Göring. Göring's leave-taking was unfriendly, to say the least. Ostensibly, he was going south so as to run the Luftwaffe from the OberSalzberg. But Hitler regarded the Luftwaffe as a failure, which had let him down badly. "The entire Luftwaffe should be hanged!" the Führer had become fond of ranting.

Himmler also left the Bunker that day. Accompanied by Walter Schellenberg, the Gestapo officer who had assumed control of his Foreign Intelligence service, the SS Reichsführer immediately paid a call on Count Folk Bernadotte, the Swedish ambassador in Berlin. Schellenberg was anxious for Himmler to play a role in the surrender of Germany and wanted him to use Bernadotte as an intermediary with Eisenhower. At this meeting, however, Himmler was not ready to do Schellenberg's bidding.

On the following day, Hitler, itching for action, ordered the Steiner attack. This was, in effect, the Nazis' last attempt to hold Berlin. Or it was supposed to be. In fact, it was the beginning of Hitler's final breakdown. The attack should have been led by SS Obergruppenführer Felix Steiner, in command of the 9th Army. But although he was still alive his army had ceased to be effective, pushed aside by the Russians. No matter how much Hitler might move around paper flags on his charts in the map room in the Bunker, Steiner could no more obey his orders than he could whistle up reinforcements from Hamburg – another of Hitler's requests.

As a result, at the conference on the next day, 22 April, there was a crisis. One news report flatly contradicted another. Down the telephone line, Himmler insisted that the Steiner attack had taken place as planned; the Luftwaffe chiefs said it hadn't. Then, while Jodl and General Hans Krebs were outlining the overall military position, definite information came at last – that the Luftwaffe had received no orders from Steiner and therefore the attack had not been carried out. This was a catastrophe, but worse news followed almost immediately. Certain troops had been moved from the north of Berlin to support Steiner in the south of the city (that much of the plan *had* gone into effect). But while they were gone, the Russians had moved down in the north to the territory vacated. The Russian forces were now *within* Berlin.

At this, Hitler cracked. He threw down the coloured pencils on to the map in front of him and erupted in a rage, shrieking at everyone. The smell of his body odour, always bad, grew worse. He blamed everyone but himself for his plight. He blamed the Luftwaffe and the army in particular, filled with "traitors and liars". Hitler's railing went on for some time and, at the end, he was exhausted. He now said something he had never uttered before. He declared that the end had come. "At last," wrote Hugh Trevor-Roper, "he despaired of his mission. All was over; the Third Reich was a failure, and its author had nothing left to do but to die. His doubts were now resolved. He would not go to the south. Anyone else who wished might go. But he would stay in Berlin and there meet the end when it came."

As usual, his Generals tried to reassure him that all was not lost and that he should leave Berlin while there was still the chance and travel south. But he would not be budged. Moreover, he insisted that the news be broadcast to the German people – that their leader was in Berlin and would stay there until the city fell.

The broadcast was duly made the following day, but by then the damage had been done inside the Bunker. After the conference broke up on 22 April, life inside was never the same again. People knew that this was the final countdown, that there was little to do other than wait for the last moves in the drama.

The break in fortune was marked. Almost immediately after the conference, Hitler set about winding up his affairs. He sent for Goebbels. Until then, the Goebbels family had lived either in their own house or in the Propaganda Ministry across Wilhelmstrasse, but Hitler now insisted that they move into the claustrophobic bunker. Each child was allowed to bring one favourite toy. For their part, Josef and Magda Goebbels insisted they would remain with the Führer – despite Hitler's orders to Goebbels that he should escape to set up a new government. Most extraordinarily, they pledged to commit suicide when the time came. Magda Goebbels', who had been in love with Hitler for years, said she would give poisoned sweets to their six children, five girls and a boy aged between four and twelve years old.

Hitler started going through his personal papers, selecting them according to those which were to be kept and those which were to be destroyed.

Later that evening he sent for Jodl and Krebs and ordered them south. When they protested, he cut them off, saying that the situation could not now be retrieved, that further orders to the troops were no longer necessary, for the situation had deteriorated beyond rescue: he added that he was planning to take over the direction of the battle in Berlin, but that he would shoot himself at the last moment. He had no intention, he said, of falling into enemy hands, alive or dead. He didn't want communists or Jews parading his corpse as a trophy.

Jodl and Krebs continued to protest but Hitler was adamant and told them that if they wanted a leader now they should look to Göring. Both men replied that neither they nor any officer in the Reich would accept an order from the Reichsmarshal. But still Hitler would not be swayed. Göring might not be a brilliant fighting general, he said, or words to that effect, but he was the right man to negotiate the surrender.

Hitler was quieter now and sat down with Field-Marshal Keitel to discuss if Berlin might still be relieved. They decided that it could if General Walther Wenck, Commander of the 12th Army which was situated south-west of Berlin on the Elbe, could turn his well-equipped forces and fight their way back to the capital via Potsdam. This would leave the British and American armies with a much easier task but it might just prevent Berlin falling to the Russians. Keitel was sent off to Wenck but only after he had eaten a dinner which Hitler provided for him. It was now 8 o'clock in the evening and Hitler sat and watched Keitel eat. By now Hitler seemed completely calm.

When he heard about Hitler's breakdown, Himmler had called the Führer and again, in a lengthy conversation, urged him to leave and fly south. Still Hitler would not be budged and such was his personal magnetism that he was not the only one. When Gottlob Berger, Commander of the SS headquarters, arrived at the Bunker very late that night to organise the evacuation of the women and children and other non-essential personnel, he found to his surprise that about half of the secretaries, telephonists and others had agreed to stay on until the very end. No pressure had been exerted; they had taken this decision of their own free will.

Berger was with Hitler when he suddenly erupted in another outburst. "Everyone has deceived me!" Hitler screamed. "No one has told me the truth! The armed forces have lied to me!" Berger said later that Hitler went on and on and on. "Then his face went bluish purple. I thought he was going to have a stroke at any minute. I had the impression that he had had a stroke already, on his left side – but of course they kept one in the dark. His arm, which a fortnight before used to jerk, was suddenly still, and he never put his left foot to the ground properly. He didn't rest his left hand properly, either, as he used to do; he only rested his right hand on the table."

Berger left the bunker at about 1 am on 23 April. That night was the last great exodus and among the evacuees were Hitler's naval Adjutant, his doctor Theo Morell and two of his four secretaries. Under Operation Seraglio, ten planes took off for Berchtesgaden.

Bormann did not go, although he wanted to. Since he had political ambitions, and the Führer was staying, he had to remain behind as well. Bormann's Adjutant, Zander, also stayed, as did his secretary, Fraulein Krueger.

At noon on Monday 23 April, General Karl Koller, Göring's Chief of Staff, reported to the Reichsmarshal the substance of the conversation Hitler had had with Jodl, the one about the Luftwaffe chief being the man to arrange the surrender. Göring was astounded but immediately aware of the delicate position he was in. By a decree signed by Hitler in June 1941, the Reichsmarshal was theoretically and legally the Führer's designated successor, but had Hitler really resigned? There was no question but that Hitler was a physical wreck and had lost his ability to think clearly or to lead but that wasn't quite the same thing as resigning.

And there was always the question of Bormann. In recent months, the Party Secretary had been in Hitler's company almost all the time and certainly more than anyone else. As a result, he had accrued great power and influence. Bormann was Göring's greatest rival. Anything Göring did would have to take account of the Party Secretary.

Accordingly, that afternoon the Reichsmarshal sent the Führer a carefully-worded telegram, asking if it was correct that he, Göring, was now meant to take over. Since the only means of communication between Berlin and the south was by radio, he added that if he had not heard back from Hitler by 10 pm, Göring would assume that the Führer had lost his freedom of action and would consider himself appointed Hitler's successor.

That same evening, Himmler held another meeting with Schellenberg and Count Bernadotte. Hitler's breakdown, the day before, had

had a great effect on Himmler, as it had on almost everyone else in the Führer's entourage. Hitherto, although Himmler thought Hitler's conduct of the War had been disastrous, his loyalty and indecision had overridden his desire to do something on his own behalf. Now he began to feel differently. Unlike some of the others, he was sure that Hitler would do as he said and remain in Berlin to the end, dying in the process. This he regarded as a release from his bond of loyalty and Himmler at last began to see himself not only as the successor to Hitler but also as Germany's saviour, the man to negotiate a just peace.

The meeting with Schellenberg and Bernadotte took place in Bernadotte's residence. They sat by candlelight because the electricity had been cut. Before the meeting could get underway an air raid took place and they were forced to go down to the cellars. It was not safe to return until after midnight. But now Himmler, after weeks of prevarication, spoke quickly. He asked Bernadotte to approach the Western Allies, through the Swedish Government, and propose a surrender. In the east, Germany would not surrender, he said, but would fight on until the Western Allies could relieve them. He wrote a personal letter for Bernadotte to take to the Swedish government as proof of his offer. He even discussed whether he should bow or shake hands when introduced to General Eisenhower.

That same evening a third important meeting was taking place, in Berlin. It was the last visit which Albert Speer was to make to Hitler. The Minister for Armaments had also heard about Hitler's breakdown and his decision to remain in the capital. Again, like Göring and Himmler, he wanted to remain loyal to the Führer and yet supercede him if the right circumstances arose.

His arrival in Berlin was adventurous, to say the least. As it was no longer possible to drive from Hamburg to Berlin, he went as far as Rechlin by car, then flew in a training plane to Gatow, the western most airfield in the capital. From there he flew on in a Fieseler Storch, a plane tiny enough to land on the East-West Axis, the great thoroughfare which dominates the centre of Berlin (and becomes Unter den Linden beyond the Brandenburg Gate).

In the Bunker, Speer found Hitler remarkably calm. Indeed, he added later that Hitler was calmer that night than at any time in the previous twelve months. He had taken his decision on his own last days and now the turmoil seemed to be over. Speer made his reckless and dangerous journey to tell the Führer about an important broadcast which he wanted to make (and had in fact already recorded in Hamburg, though it was undelivered). It was a passionate speech in which he appealed for as much as possible of Germany's material assets to be saved. Factories, bridges, dams – he wanted all these saved so that post-War reconstruction would need to be much less. He knew that presenting this plan to Hitler might be tricky. In fact, it might be a great deal more than tricky for it smacked of defeatism and Hitler could easily lash out at him or even have him shot. But still Speer went ahead.

In fact, Hitler took it well. His psychological tranquility may have had something to do with it, as might Speer's candour and the fact that Hitler had never felt let down by Speer. He also considered Speer an artist, from an artistic milieu which Hitler himself had once sought to be part of. Whatever the reason for it, the Führer treated him kindly.

Speer also saw Magda Goebbels. His account conflicts with that of others. Some said she was in love with Hitler, herself a fanatic who, in the words of Trevor-Roper, was "determined to offer up the corpses of her children on an underground cement altar . . . Only by this sacrifice . . . could she achieve any kind of triumph over the younger but childless girl" who was to become Frau Hitler in name as well as circumstance. Speer, however, said that Magda was close to total collapse and that he "didn't believe for one moment that she would have taken the decision [to commit suicide] without being bullied into it."

Speer stayed in the Bunker for about eight hours. During that time there was an Allied air raid that sent Goebbels' Propaganda Ministry up in flames. Speer used this opportunity to talk with Eva Braun, who filled him in on details of Hitler's breakdown. Speer also witnessed Goebbels and von Ribbentrop again trying to persuade Hitler to leave. Speer did not support them. He told Hitler it was more dignified to stay. Hitler reasserted his decision and further said he would not fight with the troops in case he was injured and captured by the Russians. He would stay in the Bunker, shoot himself at the last moment and have his body burned.

By then Göring's telegram had arrived in the Bunker. Bormann could not believe his luck. He had always wanted to ruin the Reichsmarshal. He showed the telegram to Hitler, stressing the passage which asked for a reply by 10 pm. This, Bormann said, was little more than an ultimatum and reminded the Führer that, about six months before, Göring had been suspected of trying to open negotiations with the Allies. Hitler had by now so fallen out with the Reichsmarshal, that

Bormann's scheming words fell on fertile ground. The Führer turned on Göring, authorising a telegram to be drafted by Bormann accusing the Reichsmarshal of high treason. The actual telegram reminded Göring that the punishment for treason was death but that in this case the punishment would not be imposed provided he resigned immediately. Göring did so next day, citing health reasons for his decision. However, that wasn't the end of the matter. Bormann had him – and his entire entourage – intercepted and kept under house arrest.

Speer left the bunker at 4 pm on 24 April. Von Ribbentrop had also left by then. Neither man was to return. Attempts were still being made by lesser lights in the Nazi hierarchy to persuade Hitler to leave. But within twenty-four hours the possibility that Hitler *could* leave had all but vanished. On 25 April, the Russians completely encircled Berlin. The siege had begun.

A word about the Bunker itself. It was situated under the gardens of the Reichschancellery and was very bleak. The ceilings were low, the passages narrow. It was not unlike being in a crypt. A few of the rooms were painted battleship grey, though the corridors were rusty brown. Some of the walls "sweated" because the masons had never finished their plastering. It was about fifty feet below ground, lined with fifteen feet of concrete with twelve or thirteen feet of earth above that. The walls were six feet thick and every time a bomb or shell landed in the Reichschancellery garden, bits of plaster and clouds of dust were dislodged. Everybody lived on top of one another and the smells were as unpleasant as the cramped conditions.

The bunker complex was divided into two (see page viii). The Bunker proper consisted of eighteen rooms. The servants' bunker was on the upper level where, after 22 April, Magda Goebbels also had a suite of four rooms.

The levels were connected by a wrought-iron spiral staircase. There was a communal general dining passage in the upper section, used by everyone except the Führer himself. All the rooms were cramped. The Bunker proper was also divided into two by a wide corridor which formed a general sitting area at one end and a conference area at the other. On one side of the passageway were the power house (power was supplied by diesel), the telephone operator, the guard's room and Goebbels' office and bedroom. On the other side was Hitler's suite, which included a separate bedroom for him and for Eva Braun, an anteroom and a map room. At the end of the passageway, by the dog bunker (guards' rest room), was a ladder which led to a concrete observation tower above the ground. This tower was unfinished.

A diesel motor in the power house, diagonally across the corridor from Hitler's suite, powered the air, water and electricity systems. In the last weeks tangled cables ran through the corridor.

Perhaps the most amazing of all, given the function of the Bunker, was the telephone exchange. Wehrmacht headquarters at Zossen, twenty miles away, had what was probably the biggest telephone exchange in Europe at that time, but in the Bunker the lines went through a relay station in the tower of the Zoo. It was hopelessly primitive and it is amazing that the Führer and his Nazi court maintained contact with the outside world for as long as they did.

There were other bunkers in the compound. For example, Bormann and the ss had one and all were connected by a series of underground passageways. Everyone lived on top of everyone else. What part this close proximity played in the events which were to unfold is difficult to gauge exactly but it must have had an effect.

That close proximity was highlighted by the very few number of people who were now living in the Bunker. Apart from guards, Trevor-Roper counted seventeen in the Bunker proper. In addition to Hitler and Eva Braun there were Josef and Magda and their six children, Hitler's valet Heinz Linge, his ss Adjutant Otto Günsche, his two loyal secretaries who hadn't left, Frau Christian and Frau Junge, his vegetarian cook Fräulein Manzialy, Gobbels's Adjutant and the very tall Ludwig Stumpfegger, Hitler's surgeon.

In the other bunkers were twenty-two senior personnel as well as guards, with a variety of functions. They included Bormann and his entourage, General Weidling, the Commandant of the city, Brigade-führer Mohnke, Commandant of the Chancellery, Artur Axmann, leader of the Hitler Youth – who were defending parts of the city – Heinz Lorenz, of the Press Service, Brigadeführer Rattenhuber, Chief of Hitler's Bodyguards and both of the Führer's personal pilots, Baur and Beetz. Many of them had been with Hitler for years and came from Bavaria. Indeed they referred to themselves as *die von dem Berg* (the mountain people). As such they thought of Hitler, and spoke of him, more as *der Chef* (the boss) than *der Führer*.

Finally, at the bottom of this cast list came the thirty or so ss security guards in the main bunker, another twenty from the other bunkers, and about 200 in all to guard the Reichschancellery.

This then was the roll call for the drama that was to be played out in the days ahead.

That night, the night of 25-26 April, there occurred an event which only underlined the unreality of the situation in the Bunker, with Hitler's health deteriorating and his contact with the outside world becoming more and more limited. Into this bizarre, highly-charged atmosphere, arrived Ritter von Greim and Hanna Reitsch. Field-Marshal Ritter von Greim was an ardent Nazi, a Luftwaffe officer with a distinguished record who commanded Luftflotte 6, with head-quarters at Munich. Hitler had sent for von Greim to promote him into the position left vacant by Göring. Von Greim's own plane had been damaged on the ground by an Allied air raid and so he flew in with Hanna Reitsch. Trevor-Roper described Reitsch as "shrill, vain, voluble," with a character well-suited to "that last subterranean mad-house in Berlin." She too was an ardent Nazi, an histrionic, flamboyant woman, who worshipped Hitler's rhetoric. But she was also an accom-plished and courageous aviatrix and together they managed to fly into Berlin against all the odds, landing on the East-West Axis, as Speer had done. Like Speer they used a Fieseler Storch, their plane blasted by anti-aircraft fire, petrol pouring from its wing tanks and their forty escort planes suffering grievous losses in the process. Von Greim was at the controls, but was wounded in the foot just before touching down, whereupon Reitsch grabbed the stick and throttle "and made a perfect landing."

On arrival at the Bunker, von Greim was immediately promoted to Field-Marshal, replacing the "treacherous" Göring as Head of the now nearly non-existent Luftwaffe. This was a formality, of course. The lives of several airmen had been sacrificed in this gesture which was made, Reitsch later recorded, with tears in the Führer's eyes.

Von Greim and Reitsch were trapped for three days in the Bunker, preventing the new Commander-in-Chief of the Luftwaffe from taking up his duties. All the planes that came to fetch them were shot down by the Russians.

The night after they arrived, Hitler summoned Hanna Reitsch to his room. "His face was lined, and his eyes were glazed by a constant film of moisture," she later wrote. The Führer told his fanatical admirer that the cause now seemed lost unless Wenck's army could return to the city and relieve it. If it could not, he said, it was his plan that he and Eva Braun would commit suicide and their bodies burned. He gave Reitsch a phial of poison for her own use, just in case she was unable to escape.

That night the Russian bombardment was especially heavy. Von

Greim and Reitsch had both decided to take the poison capsules if the Russians should break through and then, before the poison had chance to produce its effects, pull the pins on their hand grenades, blowing their dying bodies to smithereens.

While von Greim and Reitsch were still in the bunker, one man had determined not to be part of the macabre death scene that was beginning to take hold of that subterranean world. He was ss Gruppenführer Hermann Fegelein, Himmler's personal representative At Hitler's headquarters. A Bavarian, a "gentleman of the turf" at one stage, and a successful commander on the Eastern Front after he became Himmler's liaison office with Hitler, Fegelein also did his career no harm by marrying Gretl, Eva Braun's sister.

If this marks him as an opportunist, it is no more than the truth. In the Bunker Fegelein gradually distanced himself from Himmler, the more so as the latter's influence began to wane, and attached himself more and more to the Führer. This had seemed no more than sensible to begin with. But by 27 April, as Hitler and Braun confided in more and more people about their decision to commit suicide, Fegelein realised that his close family attachment to the central couple could be dangerous. He too might be expected to follow their example.

Fegelein therefore disappeared. At first his absence wasn't noticed. He didn't live in the central bunker and so was not in as close proximity to Hitler as some others. By chance – bad luck – Hitler asked to see him on the afternoon of 27 April and so learned that Fegelein was no longer where he was supposed to be. Hitler had been chronically suspicious since the Generals' Plot the previous July, when East Prussian Army Generals had smuggled in a briefcase of explosives to a conference. Miraculously, Hitler had escaped, while four men lay dead and fatally wounded around him. Later in the day on 20 July 1944, he had even met Mussolini – shaking hands with his undamaged left hand. Now, Hitler immediately ordered the ss escort to go out into the city and find Fegelein.

The search did not take long. Fegelein was found at his home in the Charlottenburg area of Berlin, dressed in civilian clothes and resting on his bed. He didn't want to return to the Reichschancellery and insisted on calling his sister-in-law in the Bunker, to ask her to intervene on his behalf. Braun refused and said he must return immediately. Fegelein was therefore marched back to the Bunker. When he arrived he was demoted from Gruppenführer and kept under armed guard.

On that night of 27-28 April, the Russian bombardment was again heavy. By all accounts, it was even more accurate so far as the Bunker was concerned and several shells landed in the Reichschancellery garden, shaking the Bunker below. According to Hanna Reitsch, Hitler gathered his entourage around him and in the heightened atmosphere rehearsed their plans for suicide "in maudlin detail". They agreed that the first appearance of Russian soldiers "would be the signal for this ritual self-sacrifice." Reitsch says that everyone present then made a speech swearing allegiance to the Führer and to Germany.

Hitler had been waiting for the relief of Berlin by Wencke's army. But by 28 April it was becoming very hard for anyone – even Hitler – to believe that Wenck would now show up. The Russians were near the centre of Berlin but still Hitler ranted. "I expect the relief of Berlin," he wired to Keitel. "Where is Wenck? What is happening to the 12th Army? When will Wenck and the 12th Army join?" All day Hitler and the others waited for news but there was none. Their ability to communicate with the outside world was diminishing – there was now only the radio-telephone to the Combined General Staff.

At 8 pm Bormann sent a bellicose telegram to Dönitz, complaining that, "instead of urging the troops forward to our rescue with orders and appeals, the men in authority are silent. Treachery seems to have replaced loyalty! We remain here. The Chancellery is already in ruins."

This was pathetic, given all that had gone before, but there was worse to come. Just on 9 o'clock that night, an official from the press service in the Propaganda Ministry brought an item of foreign news that was felt to be of special interest to those incarcerated in the Bunker. Heinz Lorenz had picked up something from the BBC. It was the news of Himmler's negotiations with Count Bernadotte regarding the surrender of German forces in the west.

When Lorenz reached the Führerbunker, he found Bormann, Goebbels and Walter Hewel – Grand-Admiral Dönitz's ambassador at Führer headquarters – sitting together. Hitler was in conference with Ritter von Greim. Lorenz therefore gave one copy of the news to them, and the other to Heinz Linge, Hitler's personal servant, to be passed on to the Führer when the conference was over.

Hanna Reitsch evocatively described the scene when Hitler found out about Lorenz's news. "He raged like a madman, his colour rose to a heated red, and his face was almost unrecognisable." This was yet more treachery and the worst example to date. Hitler now called Bormann and Goebbels into a conference behind locked doors and the last phase of the last days had begun. There can be no doubt that Hitler's discovery of Himmler's betrayal hastened the pace of the events which followed.

First he asked for Fegelein to be sent in. He, after all, was Himmler's liaison man in the Bunker and Hitler now saw – or thought he saw – how all the pieces fitted together. He assumed that Himmler had been responsible for the failure of the Steiner attack. And Fegelein's absconding had been part of an ss plot, since he was obviously aware of Himmler's meetings with Bernadotte. It was subsequently put about that Fegelein confessed to knowing about Himmler's meetings with the Swede, but it really didn't matter what Fegelein said. Hitler wanted vengeance. He was being betrayed right, left and centre but here was one of the traitors in his clutches. Fegelein was taken out into the garden of the Reichschancellery and shot.

The execution seems to have calmed Hitler for he now turned his attention to the plight of Berlin, militarily speaking. Intelligence reports confirmed that Russian tanks had reached Potsdamer Platz. Barely a block from the Vossstrasse, it was the southern limit of the Chancellery. Von Greim was instructed to ensure that every Luftwaffe plane available was dispatched to attack them.

Against this bleak background, there was one item of good news for those in the Bunker. Against all odds, a solitary plane had managed to fly into Berlin, to take von Greim back to his operational headquarters. It had circled down from a height of 13,000 feet to land on the East-West Axis. Hitler held his last meeting with von Greim shortly after midnight. He gave his new Commander-in-Chief of the Luftwaffe two orders. As he spoke his face was white and he sat on the edge of the bed. His first order was for von Greim to send every Luftwaffe plane he could lay his hands on to attack the Russian troops in Berlin. Even now Hitler still hoped that, with Luftwaffe aid, Wenck might relieve the capital. His second order was for the arrest of Himmler. "As he mentioned that name, Hitler's voice became more unsteady, and his lips and hands trembled. 'A traitor must never succeed me as Führer,' he shouted. 'You must go out to ensure that he does not!'"

Von Greim and Reitsch were minded to stay but Hitler insisted they leave while there was a chance. Reitsch took a sheaf of personal letters from the Bunker inhabitants, including items from the Goebbels family and from Eva Braun to her sister, Fegelein's widow (though no mention was made of the fate that had befallen the erstwhile Gruppenführer).

And then they left in the early hours of 29 April, Reitsch going as she had arrived, according to Trevor-Roper, "in a profusion of tears, rhetoric and abstract nouns." Though buffeted by Russian barrages, the plane reached 20,000 feet. Berlin was engulfed in flames below. They reached Rechlin in safety, where von Greim gave the Luftwaffe its orders to support the relief of Berlin. Von Greim and Reitsch then flew on to Ploen, headquarters of Dönitz.

Back in the Bunker in the early hours of 29 April, Hitler at last married Eva Braun. There had been many weird scenes in the Bunker recently but this was surely the most curious. They were married by Walter Wagner, brought there at the behest of Goebbels. Wagner was a Gau Inspector and therefore was employed by Goebbels in his capacity as Gauleiter of Berlin. As an official of the city administration he was felt to be a suitable authority, though nobody but Goebbels had ever seen him before. He wore the uniform of the Nazi Party and the armband of the Volkssturm.

The marriage only took a few minutes, carried out in the map room, which adjoined the ante-room to Hitler's suite. Goebbels and Bormann were present as witnesses. The ceremony was quickly over. Hitler and Eva Braun declared that they were of pure Aryan descent and free from any hereditary disease. It was in any case wartime and so, under German law, simple word of mouth vows were enough. As they signed the register, Eva went to write "Eva Braun", beginning her second name with a "B". She checked herself, and corrected it to "Eva Hitler, *née* Braun." Once the formalities were over, the newly-weds appeared in the central corridor, to be congratulated by waiting generals and staff, then withdrew again for a wedding breakfast. It was now between 1 and 3 am. After a short delay, Bormann, Goebbels, and Hitler's two secretaries, Frau Christian and Frau Junge, were invited into the private suite where they sat for several hours drinking champagne and chatting. "The conversation was of old times and old comrades, of Goebbels' marriage, which Hitler had witnessed, in happier days; now the position of the parties was reversed, and the happiness was reversed too."

This was a triumph of sorts for Eva Braun. She had been sent away from the Bunker, but had returned on 15 April against Hitler's will. Her loyalty had now won its just reward, or a reward of sorts.

During that wedding breakfast, things soon took another maudlin turn and Hitler spoke again of his plans for suicide. He had been betrayed by so many friends, he said, that death now would be a relief. He then adjourned to an adjoining room with Frau Junge and began to dictate his Will and also his Political Testament, which was to be his final appeal to posterity, his last attempt to justify the Nazi creed. He began this Testament by saying that he had never wanted war in 1939, that it had all been provoked by Jews or Jewish business interests. He concluded by saying that he wished to share the fate of the millions who had decided to remain in the city. "I will not fall into the hands of an enemy who requires a new spectacle, exhibited by the Jews, to divert his hysterical masses. I have therefore decided to remain in Berlin, and there to choose death voluntarily at the moment when I believe that the residency of the Führer and Chancellor can no longer be held." He went on to expel Göring and Himmler from the party and to appoint Grand-Admiral Karl Dönitz as his successor. In other words, the Luftwaffe, the Army and the ss had all betrayed him, so his successor had to come from the Navy. He specified certain ministers in the new government, not including Speer and von Ribbentrop or anyone who might have had ambitions to be the new Führer.

In his Will he still clung to the belief that his wishes would be adhered to. He asked that his belongings be given to the State and that the countless paintings he had caused to be looted all across Europe should still be used to create a fantastic museum in his home town of Linz, in Austria. Bormann was appointed executor. He ended: "my wife and I choose to die in order to escape the shame of overthrow or capitulation. It is our wish that our bodies be burnt immediately in the place where I have performed the greater part of my daily work during the course of my twelve years' service to my people."

Three copies of the Will and the Political Testament were signed at about 4 o'clock on the morning of the 29 April and witnessed. Hitler then went to bed.

Goebbels also retired, but not to sleep. He now penned his own Appendix to Hitler's Political Testament, in which he said that for the first time in his life he was to disobey an order of the Führer's. Hitler had ordered him to leave Berlin, he said, to take part in the government of the country, as a minister under Dönitz. But, said Goebbels, he preferred to stay loyal to the Führer. "For this reason, together with my wife, and on behalf of my children, who are too young to speak for themselves, but who would unreservedly agree with this decision if they were old enough, I express an unalterable resolution not to leave the Reich capital, even if it falls, but rather, at the side of the Führer, to end a life which will have no further value to me if I cannot spend it in the service of the Führer, and by his side."

It was now 5.30 am. During the day a number of couriers were sent out of the Bunker, one to Dönitz for example, one to Field-Marshal Schoener, the new Commander-in-Chief of the Army. At noon the usual situation conference was held, attended by Hitler, Bormann, Goebbels, Krebs and Voss amongst others. The conference was told that the Russians were gaining ground in all areas of the city and that there was still no news of Wenck. Immediately after the conference, General Wilhelm Burgdorf, the Adjutant of the Führer headquarters, asked Hitler's permission for a plan whereby three officers might try to get through to Wenck's army to order him to hurry. Hitler agreed and, shortly afterwards, Freytag von Loringhoven, Gerhardt Boldt and Lieutenant Colonel Weiss left the Bunker.

By the 4 o'clock conference that day, the situation had deteriorated still further. Seeing that three officers had been allowed to go that afternoon, Colonel Nicolaus von Below, Hitler's air force Adjutant, now asked if he too might leave. Hitler agreed, but asked von Below to wait until the ten o'clock conference, after which he wanted to send another document out of the Bunker. This conference was attended by General Karl Weidling, the Commandant of the city. Weidling described in grim detail how the situation had continued to worsen, much as they had all expected. The Russians had advanced in the Saarlandstrasse and the Wilhelmstrasse almost as far as the Air Ministry. There were many other Russian successes too, he said, and their forces would surely reach the Reichschancellery by 1 May at the latest. All knew the significance of May Day in the Communist calendar.

After this conference, Hitler's postscript to his Testament was handed to von Below by Burgdorf. It was addressed to Field-Marshal Wilhelm Keitel, one of the generals who had always played up to the Führer. It was Hitler's valediction to the German Armed Forces. He again denounced Göring and Himmler and repeated his intention to commit suicide. He praised the Navy, now excused the Luftwaffe – it had done its best but had been let down by Göring – but he excoriated the Army, especially the Generals who had resisted him and conspired against them the previous summer.

Then Hitler took his leave of von Below. They shook hands but did not speak. Von Below and his batman left just on midnight of 29-30 April. They were the last people to leave the Bunker before the end.

Throughout the day of 29 April, the mood below ground had been macabre and sombre. It had not been helped by the fact that, during the afternoon, Hitler had had his favourite Alsatian, Blondi, destroyed. The dog had been poisoned by Professor Haase, a former surgeon to the Führer, as an illustration of what cyanide could do and how quickly it acted. Nor was the mood helped when Hitler gave his two remaining secretaries poison capsules in case they should decide they needed them. This was hardly the best of parting gifts, Hitler remarked as he praised their courage.

There was, however, a strange change of mood that took place about 3 o'clock on the morning of 30 April. During dinner the previous evening in the upper bunker, word had come through that Hitler wished to bid farewell to all the ladies in his entourage. Everyone was forbidden to retire until that had happened. At about 2.30 am, Hitler walked through from his own private quarters, accompanied by Bormann. "His look was abstracted, his eyes glazed over with that film of moisture which Hanna Reitsch had noticed." He made no speech but walked silently down the line, shaking hands with everyone. When others spoke to him, he merely mumbled in reply and then took his leave.

After he had gone, there was for a short moment a muted silence among those people who had been present. All realised that the ceremony they had just been part of could herald only one thing: Hitler's suicide was imminent.

And that is when the change of mood took place. "A great and heavy cloud seemed to roll away from the spirits of the Bunker-dwellers," said Trevor-Roper. Incredible as it may seem in the circumstances, a dance was organised in the canteen. People got drunk. The divisions of rank broke down, the noise level rose and even when word came from the Führerbunker for the revellers to be quiet, they took no notice. It was as if some sort of dam had burst.

Later in the morning of Monday 30 April, the military situation improved a fraction. The Schlesischer railway station had been re-captured from the Russians. But by noon this small gain had been more than wiped out. The Russians had seized the underground railway tunnel in the Friedrichstrasse, they had the whole of the Tiergarten, were across the River Spree at the Weidendammer bridge and were in the tunnel under the Vossstrasse. They were very close to the Reichschancellery.

Hitler was still calm and took all this news with no show of feeling. He ate lunch at about 2 o'clock. Eva Braun was not there and so he sat with his two secretaries and his cook, as usual in these circumstances. During lunch, the final rites were put into effect. Hitler's ss Adjutant, Otto Günsche, sent an order to his chauffeur Erich Kempka for 200 litres of petrol to be brought to the Chancellery garden. At such short notice, Kempka was able to find only about 180 litres, but that was brought in jerry cans carried by four men. The cans were placed on the ground just outside the emergency exit of the Bunker. Everyone peripheral to the drama about to be enacted was then ordered away from the Chancellery.

After lunch Hitler remained behind in his suite for a short while. When he emerged, he was accompanied by Eva Braun, who wore a blue dress. Now another farewell ceremony took place. Present this time were all the most important people in the Bunker: Bormann, Goebbels, Burgdorf, Krebs, Hewel, Naumann, Voss, Rattenhuber, Hoegl, Günsche, Linge and the four women, Frau Christian, Frau Junge, Fräulein Krueger and Fräulein Manzialy, the cook. Magda Goebbels was not there. As the death of her six children approached, she preferred to remain in her own room.

Hitler and his new wife shook hands with the others and then returned to their own suite. Only a few of the others remained in the passageway outside – exactly *who* was to form one of the great mysteries later on. After a short delay, "a single shot was heard. After an interval they entered the suite. Hitler was lying on the sofa, which was soaked with blood. He had shot himself through the mouth. Eva Braun was also on the sofa, also dead. A revolver was by her side, but she had not used it; she had swallowed poison. The time was half past three."

Both Artur Axmann and Erich Kempka claim to have entered the Bunker shortly after Hitler's death. And Axmann, at least, was in the room when Linge wrapped the Führer's body in a blanket, to conceal his bloodstained and shattered head. Linge carried the body out into the passage "where the others easily recognised it by the familiar black trousers." Linge passed the body to two other ss officers who lifted it up the four flights of stairs to the emergency exit and out into the garden.

Meanwhile, Bormann had entered the room where the suicide had taken place, and taken the body of Eva Braun. "Her death had been tidier and no evidence had been needed to conceal evidence of it." Her body was passed along, from Bormann, to Kempka, to Günsche, to a third SS officer who followed his colleagues up to the garden.

Precautions had been taken so that as few people as possible would witness the last scenes. The doors linking the main Bunker with the other ones had been locked and as many people as possible ordered away from the area. Despite this, there were two unofficial witnesses to what happened next. One was Erich Mansfeld, on duty in the concrete observation tower at the corner of the Bunker. The other was Hermann Karnau, who should have left the Chancellery with the rest but had stayed behind and was standing in the garden near the observation tower.

Mansfeld saw the two SS officers carrying a body with a blanket covering its upper half and black trousers emerging below. He also saw the third SS officer carrying the "unmistakeable" corpse of Eva Braun, followed by the figures of Bormann, Goebbels, Günsche and Linge.

Karnau arrived on the scene a little later. The first thing he noticed were two bodies lying side by side on the ground of the Chancellery garden and near the emergency exit of the Bunker. Almost immediately, the two bodies appeared to burst into flame, something he couldn't at first explain. Mansfeld, however, could. The corpses had been laid side by side and doused in petrol from the jerry cans that Kempka had organised. But before they could be set alight, a Russian artillery barrage had forced everyone back under the lintel of the emergency exit to the Bunker. So from there, Günsche had dipped a piece of rag in petrol, set fire to it and thrown the lighted taper on to the corpses which immediately burst into flame. "The mourners stood to attention, gave the Hitler salute, and withdrew again into the Bunker, where they dispersed."

Karnau watched the corpses burn for a little while, then followed the others into the bunker. Mansfeld, in the tower, also continued to watch. He saw other SS officers come into the garden a little later and pour more petrol on to the corpses, to keep them alight. Shortly after that he was relieved by Karnau and now the two of them went to inspect the corpses close up. "By now the lower parts of both bodies had been burned away and the shin-bones of Hitler's legs were visible." Mansfeld went back a third time, an hour later. The bodies were still burning but the flame was low.

It was not until after dark, after a delay of maybe six or even seven hours that Brigadeführer Johann Rattenhuber gave the order for the bodies to be buried, threatening the guards he had chosen to keep their "holy secret" on pain of death by shooting. The ever-alert Mansfeld returned to his observation post shortly before midnight. By the light of the flares being used by the Russians to illuminate Berlin, he noticed that the two bodies had disappeared but that a bomb crater in the front of the emergency exit for the Bunker had been newly worked over, with the earth around the edges piled up neatly. He had absolutely no doubt that this is where Hitler and Braun had been buried.

And that is where Trevor-Roper concluded his account. "That is all that is known about the disposal of the remains of Hitler's and Eva Braun's bodies," he wrote. And then he added this: "Linge afterwards told one of the secretaries that they had been burned, as Hitler had ordered, 'till nothing remained'; but it is doubtful whether such total combustion could have taken place. 180 litres of petrol, burning slowly on a sandy bed, would char the flesh and dissipate the moisture of the bodies, leaving only an unrecognisable and fragile remainder; but the bones would withstand the heat. These bones have never been found."

That last sentence was no more than the truth but it was a fact that would undermine much of the *raison d'être* of Trevor-Roper's investigation – to lay to rest speculation about Hitler's fate once and for all. For notwithstanding the confident tone in which Trevor-Roper's conclusions were couched, in the absence of the Hitler's corpse there soon sprang up a great deal of doubt about his end.

Before we explore all that, however, there is one further aspect of Trevor-Roper's report that we need to consider, albeit briefly. This is the death of the Goebbels family, an act which, even after all this time, must still rank as the most ghoulish occurrence that took place in the Bunker. We need to understand this because it is somewhat more important to the overall story than has hitherto been acknowledged. Goebbels' decision to end his life after Hitler's had been taken long before. As we have seen, he had even published his intentions in his Appendix to the Führer's Testament. On the day after Hitler's death, the moment to fulfill those intentions had at last arrived. He retired to his own quarters and for a while received visitors. The children were killed first, given poisoned chocolate, it was said with the help of Dr Haase. Later, Goebbels commandeered Gunther Schwaegermann, his Adjutant, to promise that he would burn their bodies after they were all dead. Magda Goebbels now made her goodbyes while Schwaegermann sent out of the Bunker for yet more petrol. Goebbels intended to copy Hitler even in the manner of his death.

The Propaganda Minister and his wife then walked through the main passage of the Bunker. At the foot of the stairs to the emergency exit they passed Schwaegermann and Rach, a driver. Without a word the couple climbed the stairs to the garden. It was 8.30 in the evening.

Soon after, Schwaegermann and Rach heard two shots and rushed to the top of the stairs. They found both Goebbels and Magda Goebbels dead on the ground, with the SS orderly who had shot them still standing nearby. Four cans of petrol were poured over the bodies and set alight. Then Schwaegermann and the others left. On their way through the Bunker, they met Brigadeführer Mohnke, commandant of the Reichschancellery, who ordered them to set the Bunker on fire. They had one can of petrol left, emptied it as best they could in the conference passage, and set it alight. "Then they left the Führer-Bunker, for it was 9 o'clock and the mass escape from the New Chancellery was due to begin."

The mass break-out need not concern us too much, save for the fact that Martin Bormann was one of those who tried to worm his way through the Russian lines. The fact that he did not do so, and that his body, or at least his skull, was not found for many years, helped the rumours to grow that Bormann definitely – and Hitler maybe – were still alive and planning a political and military revival.

Just as the Western Allies had been obsessed by the possibility of a National Redoubt during the last months of the war, so the first years of peace saw an equal concern with any possible resurgence by the Nazis. The rapid development of the Cold War did little to help matters, breeding as it did a climate of suspicion and secrecy. This was aided by the fact that several leading Nazis – Otto Skorzeny, General Gehlen, SS Colonel Adolf Eichmann, Joseph Mengele – had managed to avoid capture.

In October 1945, 200 copies of a public notice were spread across Germany, which read in part: "Martin Bormann is charged with having committed crimes against peace, war crimes and crimes against humanity . . . If Martin Bormann appears, he is entitled to be heard." This was the work of the International Military Tribunal at Nuremberg. The deputy chief prosecutor, Sir David Maxwell-Fyffe, said to the President of the Tribunal that "there is still the possibility that he is alive."

By 1946, the US Treasury Department was aware that Bormann had directed an intricate plan for the distribution of funds through foreign companies, 750 in all, 200 in the Iberian peninsular, thirty-five in Turkey, ninety-eight in Argentina, 214 in Switzerland, many with research institutions near lakes and hydro-power plants so that engineers of the Fourth Reich had the camouflage of scientific inquiry to cover their financial hoarding. A special organisation, or escape route – *die Spinne* (the Spider) – operated routes from Hamburg to Rome overland and Hamburg to Genoa by sea. Distribution centres were located at fifty-mile intervals along this web. Spain was particularly attractive as a first port of call because, as Allied Intelligence had noted, the Madrid station for military Intelligence had 357 full-time agents, a large permanent staff, together with provision to pay no fewer than 890 Spanish locals. It was clearly a front for something else. Switzerland was next. A list was obtained which showed that there were 20,000 "safe houses" there "where Nazi collaborators could catch their breath and plan the transfer of funds for a possible Fourth Reich."

Another route lay through Yugoslavia. During the war the Partisans in occupied Yugoslavia managed to observe much Nazi activity within their shifting borders and beyond. For example, Slav Partisans had watched the Germans removing paintings and other treasures in the ObserSalzberg and were aware that the Americans did not find everything when they arrived in May 1945. And Ante Pavelic, a Yugoslav collaborator who had been forced to flee at the War's end, was known to have been picked up by ODESSA's couriers, taken to Spain, and given a new identity for Latin America. Pavelic ended up in Paraguay in the same restricted zone that housed Joseph Mengele.

There were many more reports of this nature throughout the late 1940s. For example, a joint project of the Ministry of Economic Warfare in Britain, and the Treasury in the US known as "Safehaven", had tracked the movement of gold, paintings, jewellery and other valuables out of Germany and into allegedly "neutral" countries during the war, and the Western Allies were well aware of the build-up of resources in South America and the part played in all this by certain central and South American politicians, such as Arnulfo Arias, president of Panama.

Just as extraordinary as the myths of a Fourth Reich led by Hitler or Bormann were Russian claims over the Führer.

During 1945, the Russians issued three categoric statements. The first came from Marshal Georgi Zhukov, Commander of the 1st Belorussian Front, one of the three Russian armies that invaded Germany.

Speaking for the Russian military command in Berlin, on 9 June he said, "We have not identified the body of Hitler ... He could have flown away from Berlin at the very last moment." The next remark came from Stalin himself. Just over a month later at the Potsdam Conference on 16 July the Soviet General Secretary said aloud to President Truman, James Byrne, the US Secretary of State and to Admiral William D. Leahy, the President's Chief of Staff, what he had already been whispering to American officials in Moscow: he believed Hitler was alive and probably living in Spain or Argentina.

But all this paled alongside an official Soviet statement issued in September that year, the very month that Trevor-Roper was commissioned to begin his inquiries that led to *The Last Days of Hitler*. "No trace of the bodies of Hitler or Eva Braun had been discovered," said the report. "... It is established that Hitler, by means of false testimony, sought to hide his traces. Irrefutable proof exists that a small airplane left the Tiergarten at dawn on 30 April flying in the direction of Hamburg. Three men and a woman are known to have been on board. It has also been established that a large submarine left Hamburg before the arrival of the British forces. Mysterious persons were on board the submarine, among them a woman."

This statement was partly designed to embarrass the British because the Hamburg-Kiel area of northern Germany was a British responsibility. But Stalin's perfidy went wider than that. Having linked the submarine escape with Hitler and Eva Braun, he subsequently told Harry Hopkins in Moscow that he believed *Bormann*, not Hitler, had got away in the U-boat. What was going on?

What was going on was a Russian obsession with Hitler no less profound than that in the West. But with a rather different purpose.

3

1968: THE RUSSIAN BOMBSHELL

In the fifty years since World War Two ended Hugh Trevor-Roper's book, *The Last Days of Hitler,* has been into seven editions, the most recent planned for release to coincide with the half-century anniversary of the end of hostilities, in spring 1995. This is a measure of the enduring interest in Hitler, and his death, and of the mystery which has continued to surround those events in the bunker in the last days of the War. This mystery is due in no small part to the Russians who, for reasons of their own, kept what they knew secret for many years and then allowed little bits of information to be released piecemeal. The last pieces of this jigsaw are only now slotting into place for the first time now, here in Chapter 5 of this book. Perhaps they will provide the last word on Hitler, the final full stop on World War Two.

From the very earliest days of peace, the Western Allies were aware that the Russians *were* making their own investigations into Hitler's fate. From Trevor-Roper's research into the break-out, the mass exodus which took place on the evening of 1 May 1945, he knew that Mohnke, Günsche, Hewel, Voss, Baur plus three secretaries and the cook had been the first to leave, followed by the rest in groups of four or five at intervals after that. Bormann, Trevor-Roper was told, was in one of these groups. Three men – Krebs, Burgdorf and Hauptsturm-führer Franz Schedle, Commander of the SS Bodyguard – preferred to wait behind and shoot themselves when the Russians entered the Chancellery.

Trevor-Roper detailed the adventures of the escaping "mountain people," and they need not detain us here. He ended with an explanation of the fate of each. Kempka, Schwaegermann, Axmann all made it to the West and to captivity, as did von Loringhoven and Boldt. Hoegl was killed. Trevor-Roper wasn't sure of Beetz (Hitler's second pilot) or of Weiss – either may have been killed or captured by the Russians. Johannmeier and Zander had both made it to the West, but had disappeared. (They were later captured, thanks to the fact that Lorenz, the press secretary, talked.) Von Below also went west, reaching Bonn. Himmler committed suicide by cyanide as soon as he was recognised by the British while he was trying to pass himself off as a nondescript soldier.

That left Mohnke, Linge, Günsche, Baur, Hewel and Rattenhuber. Trevor-Roper found that they had been captured by the Russians, along with four of the female secretaries. He'd found this out because the women had been released and three of them had moved West, telling the Allies this story in the process. They'd also revealed that Baur was seriously wounded and that all the men seemed determined to commit suicide. Trevor-Roper concluded that "they may well have done so".

However, these facts were never confirmed officially by the Russians and, at the time of Trevor-Roper's November 1945 press conference, the Western Allies were not very much wiser. He told the conference that he knew the Russians had dug up about 160 bodies in the garden of the Reichschancellery and that he believed that they had found "two sets of teeth. They got hold of a woman who was assistant to Hitler's dentist, and asked her if they were Hitler's teeth. After interrogation, she said she recognised them as Hitler's teeth."

So far as Hitler's bodily remains were concerned, that was it. The Cold War was now developing and, from the Soviets, there came no word about what they had. After the statement issued in September – to the effect that they believed Hitler had escaped by submarine (the version which later had Bormann playing the main role) – Russian official policy appeared to be that Hitler's fate was of no importance to them. As W. Byford-Jones put it in his 1963 book, *Berlin Twilight*: "It was also obvious that the Russians must have salvaged from the chancellery and from the bunker important documents, not all of which were sent forward for inclusion in their case for the prosecution at the War Criminals' trial at Nuremburg." Byford-Jones also happened to mention something that took place in August 1945 when he had visited Hitler's Bunker along with a Russian friend. "An insignificant block of concrete, inlet with substantial steel doors, the hinges of which had been burned off with acetylene blow-lamps, led down to Hitler's elaborate air-raid shelter, so deep below ground that no bomb used in Europe could have penetrated its walls ... We went down several flights of steps into the dark Bunker, where Hitler lived during the fateful days ... The timber was scorched black, the floor was covered with three inches of water . . . No fire had burned in Hitler's room, a room in which, according to reports, Hitler and Eva Braun had spent a Wagnerian honeymoon . . . On a broad settee, its upholstery covered with brocade decorated with leaping antelopes and mediaeval warriors in Russian top-boots, there were clear signs of blood.

"My Russian friend and I examined the settee carefully. The signs were consistent with someone who sat in the corner of it having committed suicide by shooting, for the blood had run down the three-inch square arm of the settee and dripped on to the floor, where there were dark stains. On the wall were several splashes of blood, which could have been accounted for by a wounded head having come into contact with it."

The Western Allies did make some efforts to find out what the Russians had. The Americans made an approach and at one point the British military commander in Berlin, Brigadier-General Fort, asked his opposite number, General Siniev, for the dental records Trevor-Roper had referred to at the press conference. Silence.

This was particularly galling because the British had captured Professor Hugo Blaschke, Hitler's dentist, and confiscated the dental records of both the Führer and Eva Braun; the Americans had captured Dr Theo Morell, who had treated Hitler in the Bunker and in whose files X-rays of Hitler's skull were found. Either of these records could have been used to confirm whether or not the teeth in Russia were those of Adolf Hitler.

Instead, there was stalemate for ten years. Then in October 1955 near Göttingen, on the border between East and West Germany, a chink appeared in the Iron Curtain. On 8 October, the Russians handed back the first large group of prisoners of war. 790 people arrived at the special displaced-persons camp at Friedland, drawing crowds from all over West Germany, anxious to find their relatives. Among this first batch were two who were of special interest, relatives or not. They were Heinz Linge, Hitler's valet, and Hans Baur, his pilot. Both had been in the Bunker.

By rights, their reappearance ought to have cleared up any lingering doubts about Hitler's death. As we have seen, Trevor-Roper's account had been based primarily on the testimony of Erich Kempka, Hitler's driver – who hadn't actually been in the Bunker when the suicide occurred – and on the testimony of Frau Junge and Frau Christian, who had both been told the vital details by others. In contrast, Baur and Linge especially had allegedly seen all. And there was the added bonus that within the Soviet penal system, neither man had had a chance to read or learn of the Western accounts. Here seemed to be the perfect opportunity to put the Trevor-Roper version to the test and settle the remaining doubts.

In fact, the water was muddied even further. Trevor-Roper had failed to mention that Baur was even in the Bunker at the crucial time. Now the ex-pilot told the waiting newsmen that he had shaken hands with *der Chef* immediately before Hitler shot himself. He implied that, excluding Eva Braun, he had been the last to see and speak to Hitler. Baur also said that Eva Braun shot herself, in flat contradiction to what Trevor-Roper had concluded.

Linge's own account was published in English in the *News of the World* on Sunday 23 October 1955. He now claimed that Hitler had given him a last instruction, to make sure the bodies were burned beyond recognition and that Linge should join the break-out groups rather than remain behind, "in order to serve who comes after me". He went on to say that after saluting the Führer his nerve suddenly went and he ran away, through the Bunker, so that he wouldn't hear the "fatal, final shot". After a moment, however, he took control of himself and returned. But not even this was straightforward. Linge claimed to have gone back not to Hitler's suite but to the map room. Outside there, he said, he never heard a shot but "I noticed [a] whiff of smoke."

This was curious, because although next to the anteroom to Hitler's suite, the map room did not lead through to it. Was this a simple error? It might be, but Linge had had ten years in Russian jails to think it all through. And the whiff of smoke?

These changes in testimony seemed doubly significant because he was now the second person to change his story. Trevor-Roper's main source, Erich Kempka, had also altered his testimony. Kempka had first been interviewed by journalists on *Life* magazine, when he had claimed that Eva Braun had shot herself through her heart and Hitler had shot himself through the right temple. By the time he was interviewed by Trevor-Roper, Kempka was saying that Braun had died from cyanide poisoning. As *The Last Days of Hitler* put it, "Kempka, who carried out the body of Eva Braun, unblanketed, observed no signs of blood."

Anyone with any experience of trial proceedings will know by just how much eyewitnesses can differ in their accounts of the same set of events. But in this case that wasn't the only – even the main – worry. It was now in the mid-1950s, after the release of Linge, Baur and others, that a suspicion began to grow that these witnesses were *deliberately* giving confusing accounts, for their own ends. What those ends might be was anyone's guess. Several of them might have been trying to make themselves out as more important than they actually had been, either for financial gain or for an unwarranted place in the history books. For the conspiracy-minded, there was always the suspicion that the confusing picture was deliberately designed to entice the thought that, maybe, after all, Hitler wasn't dead.

Sightings of Hitler had dropped off by now (though they were to continue until the early 1990s in some form or another!). But the fascination with the man and his final hours continued and a fresh controversy erupted in the 1960s. Some hint of what was to come appeared in 1965 in an article in a Russian politico-literary journal, *Znamya*, by a woman who had been attached to the fifteen-strong Red Army *Sonderkommand* charged with finding Hitler. In this article, entitled *Berlinskii Stranitsy* (Berlin Notes), she referred to a certain number of documents confirming that the Russians *had* carried out substantial inquiries at the end of the War.

Perhaps this article (and a book which followed it) persuaded the Soviet authorities that the time was ripe to release part of their story. Whatever the reason, a well known Russian journalist, Lev Bezymenski, who had served in the Red Army in both Stalingrad and Berlin, published a book in West Germany in 1968, then in London and New York, called *The Death of Adolf Hitler*. This book, barely a hundred pages long, was a bombshell.

Bezymenski began in this fashion. "It would be senseless exaggeration to say that the Soviet Army battled for Berlin merely because Adolf Hitler was there. It had other, more important, goals. This may explain why Soviet historical writing has so far paid little attention to Hitler's final fate. But it was only natural that, simultaneously with the attack on Berlin, the question was raised of where War Criminal Number One might be."

Bezymenski let it be known that the Russians had forced Linge and Günsche to write their own accounts of those last few days. This provided a vivid and, on the face of it, authoritative alternative to – or corroboration of – Trevor-Roper's narrative.

Linge's account began on 21 April. "Hitler was roused at about 9.30 am, and told that Berlin was in the line of fire of Russian artillery. Burgdorf as well as other adjutants waited for him in the ante-chamber. Ten minutes later, Hitler, unshaven, hastily entered the ante-chamber. As a rule he did his own shaving. Not even his personal barber, August Wollenhaupt, was allowed to shave him; he said that he could not bear to have anyone with a razor operate close to his throat [Hitler had been like this ever since the attempt on his life in July 1944]."

Hitler wanted to know where all the shooting and cacophony was coming from. Burgdorf told him that the centre of Berlin was under fire from a Russian battery that appeared to be situated northwest of Zossen: "Hitler went white. 'Are the Russians that close?'"

The next day the bombardment increased and the Führer was awake as early as 9 am. (He usually did not get up until midday, working late until 4 or so the following morning.) A military conference was called for noon. "It was the shortest military conference of the entire war," wrote Linge. "Many of the faces were distorted. In muffled voices, the same question was repeated over and over again: 'Why can't the Führer make up his mind to leave Berlin?'

"Hitler came from his private rooms, his stoop seeming more pronounced than ever. He greeted the members of the conference casually and almost fell into his chair. General Krebs started to outline the situation, reporting a considerable deterioration.

"Hitler raised himself out of his chair and bent down over the table. He started to point to something on the map, his hands shaking. Suddenly he straightened up and threw his coloured pencils on to the table. He drew a deep breath, his face became flushed, his eyes opened wide. He took a step back from the table and in a breaking voice shrieked: 'That's the end! Under such circumstances I cannot direct anything any more! The War is lost! But you are mistaken, gentlemen, if you think I will leave Berlin! I'd rather put a bullet through my head!'

"Everyone stared at him in horror. He barely lifted his hand. 'Thank you gentlemen!' Then he left the room."

Hitler's ss Adjutant Günsche had followed Hitler back into his quarters. After a moment or two, he returned to the others. Keitel and Bormann questioned the adjutant on what Hitler had said. He had asked to speak to Goebbels and was on the phone to him now. "They all talked at once and interrupted each other. Keitel excitedly waved his hands, Bormann seemed beside himself and repeated ceaselessly: 'It's impossible, the Führer can't really want to shoot himself!' Keitel screamed: 'We have to stop the Führer!' The chaos was indescribable.

Some poured themselves brandy from the bottle that stood on the table.

"Around 12.30 Goebbels arrived in the ante-chamber, limping in extreme agitation: 'Where is the Führer?' He was immediately led into Hitler's study. The conference between Hitler and Goebbels lasted about ten minutes. As Goebbels came out of the room, Bormann, Keitel, Dönitz and Jodl rushed up to him: 'What did the Führer say?' They surrounded him, and Goebbels told them that Hitler considered the situation hopeless, he saw no more possibilities and thought the war was lost. He had broken down completely, never before had he seen him in such a state. Goebbels related, further, how shocked he had been when Hitler had told him, over the telephone, in a breaking voice, that he and his wife and children should move immediately into the Führerbunker, since this was the end."

Although this statement was not published until 1968, remember it had been actually made in 1945 when Linge could have had no knowledge of what Trevor-Roper was being told by Frau Christian, Frau Krueger and Eric Kempka.

Later, Bezymenski's account confirmed that General Krebs had approached General Chuikov, head of the Russian forces attacking Berlin at around dawn on 1 May, asking for a negotiated surrender and informing him of Hitler's suicide. This offer was refused. The next day, Bezymenski said, Otto Günsche had been arrested "and his copious testimony regarding the Führer's death became available. He had, however, been caught on the outskirts of the city . . . and his testimony became known only much later. Some people had been taken prisoner in the immediate vicinity of the Chancellery, but their testimony about Hitler's death was very vague."

Inside the Reichschancellery itself, the job of investigating Hitler's whereabouts fell to Lieutenant-Colonel Ivan Isayevich Klimenko, Commander of the Counter Intelligence Section, 79th Rifle Corps, and part of the Third Shock Army. The Chancellery had actually been stormed the night before, by soldiers of the 5th Shock Army.

Klimenko's account to Bezymenski was made in the 1960s. He claimed that he and his colleagues had at first been stationed at Plötzensee Prison, where captured soldiers were being taken. There, he heard from several of the people they arrested early that day, that both Hitler and Goebbels had committed suicide actually inside the Chancellery. Klimenko had therefore decided to take four witnesses with him and drive there.

"It was afternoon and it rained. I climbed into a jeep, the witnesses and soldiers into an army truck. We drove up to the Chancellery, went into the garden, and arrived at the emergency exit of the Führerbunker. As we approached this exit, one of the Germans shouted: 'That is Goebbels' corpse! That is the corpse of his wife!'

"I decided to take these corpses with us. Since we did not have a stretcher, we placed the corpses on an unhinged door, manoeuvred them on to the truck (it was a covered vehicle), and returned to Plötzensee.

"The day after, 3 May 1945, the corpses of six Goebbels children and the corpse of General Krebs were found in the Bunker. They too were taken to Plötzensee . . .

"Goebbels' body was laid in a room on the table, the bodies of his wife and children and that of General Krebs were put on the floor. The witnesses were kept in another room. The first to enter the room was Vice-Admiral Voss, the representative of Grand-Admiral Dönitz at Führer headquarters; he had been captured by members of the Counter Intelligence Section of the 3rd Shock Army. Without hesitation he identified Goebbels and his children. The other witnesses did the same.

"Goebbels death was proved beyond any doubt . . . Naturally we asked Voss where Hitler might be. Voss gave no clear answer and told us only that he had left Berlin together with Hitler's adjutant [Günsche], who had told him that Hitler had committed suicide and that his corpse had been burned in the Chancellery garden." Klimenko decided that another visit to the Chancellery was called for.

He took Voss, an interpreter and a subordinate. Inside the Bunker, he found that Voss behaved "somewhat strangely; he was nervous, mumbling unintelligibly." It was dark in the Bunker, they didn't find much, and worked their way back into the garden by the emergency exit. "It was close to 9 pm. We stepped up to a big, dried-up water tank for fire-fighting. It was filled with many corpses. 'Here,' Voss said, pointing to a corpse: 'Oh, this is Hitler's body!'

"This corpse was dressed, the feet were in mended socks. After a moment Voss began to have his doubts: 'No, no, I can't say with certainty that it is Hitler.' Frankly I also had my doubts because of the mended socks!" [Hitler was known to be a meticulous and scrupulous dresser.]

This was an unsatisfactory set of circumstances and so Klimenko searched in Plötzensee prison for people who had known Hitler

The main hall of the ruined Reichschancellery in 1945. The Russians announced their intention to build a war memorial in honour of Stalin and the Russian soldiers who had been killed in the battle for Berlin

Marshal Zhukov on the steps of the Reichstag, May 1945

One of the last known photographs of Adolf Hitler, awarding the Iron Cross to Alfred Czech, a twelve-year-old Hitler Youth soldier. Under Artur Axsmann's command, the Hitler Youth defended parts of Berlin

The emergency exit of the Bunker, as photographed by the first Russian commission, with a key added to the most important locations: x indicates the burial spot of the bodies of Hitler and his wife Eva Braun on 30 Apr 1945; xx is the area where the corpses were partially burned; and xxx shows the doorway down from the garden into the Bunker itself. The photograph was taken from a Russian film

Soviet Minister of the Interior, Lavrenti Beria (holding his hat) and Foreign Minister Vyacheslav Mikhailovich Molotov (in a Trilby) visiting the Bunker in May 1945. The ruined watertower in the background hid the body of Hitler's doppelänger

An American GI in Hitler's private suite in the Bunker, January 1946

The narrow bed in the Führer's bedroom. The trickle of blood on the wooden support *(lower right)* led to theories about Hitler's last hours being reconsidered

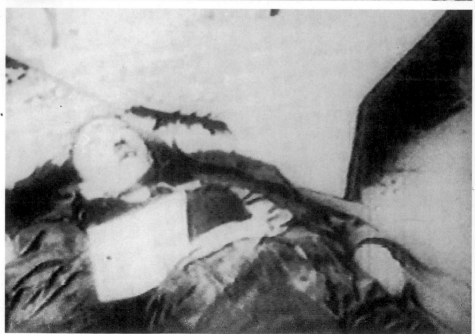

Gustav Weler, Hitler's double, at first thought by the Russian forces to be the Führer himself. He had been shot in the forehead

The charred corpse of Josef Goebbels, his arm jack-knifed as if in a Nazi salute. His wife Magda, lies beyond

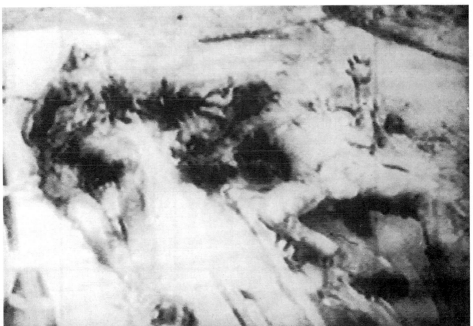

Magda *(left)* and Josef Goebbels. His clenched fingers can be clearly seen. Their six children – aged between four and twelve years old – were found poisoned inside the Bunker

Adolf Hitler's upper jaw and
(right) his lower jaw, showing teeth
and bridgework. The Führer's
dental records played a crucial part
in Russian identification of the
body

Hitler's other remains, gathered together in an ammunition box. They form part of the Operation Myth File,
the Hitler archive inside the Kremlin, Moscow

Marshal Georgi Zhukov signs the unconditional surrender on 8 May 1945

Field-Marshal Wilhelm Keitel *(seated, far end of table)* signs the surrender on behalf of defeated Germany

General Vassili Ivanovich Chuikov, the Russian commander to whom General Hans Krebs tried to surrender in April 1945

Below: British Prime Minister Winston Churchill, American President Harry Truman and Soviet Secretary Joseph Stalin at the Potsdam Conference, July 1945. Stalin tried to convince his allies that Hitler was alive and living in Spain

personally. He says he found half a dozen during the next day or so, but gives no names. At around 11 am on 4 May, he took these prisoners back to the Chancellery – only to find that the all-important body had been moved. By now the Chancellery building was part of the headquarters for the 5th Shock Army and it took Klimenko a while to gain the necessary entry documents. Once inside, however, he soon found the corpse with the darned socks, laid out with others. "Only one of the six witnesses said it might be Hitler. The other five denied it categorically."

This too was far from satisfactory. A Soviet diplomat who knew Hitler was sent for, but while they were waiting someone voiced the thought, "Where was Goebbels found?" Without waiting for the Soviet diplomat to show up, Klimenko took his team back to the garden, near the emergency exit.

"Private Ivan Chiurakov climbed into a nearby crater that was strewn with burned paper. I noticed a bazooka in there and called to Chiurakov: 'Climb out quickly, or you may be blown to bits!' Chiurakov answered: 'Comrade Lieutenant Colonel, there are legs here!'"

Two bodies were pulled out from the crater, a man and a woman. "Of course, at first I didn't even think that these might be the corpses of Hitler and Eva Braun, since I believed that Hitler's corpse was already in the Chancellery and only needed to be identified. I therefore ordered the corpses to be wrapped in blankets and reburied."

The diplomat eventually arrived. He was in Berlin in expectation of the end of the War and possible surrender. He was the only man among all the forces in Berlin who had met the Führer. When he arrived in the Chancellery, he was accompanied by several generals. It was about 2 in the afternoon but he quickly disappointed his entourage, confirming that the body with the darned socks was *not* Hitler. "You can safely bury him . . ."

This prompted Klimenko to reconsider Churakov's find. Early on 5 May he returned to the crater and, with two other officers, dug up the corpses they had reburied the previous day. In the course of their excavations this time around, they also found the remains of two dogs.

An autopsy was to be performed on these corpses but, before that had happened, Soviet patrols in Berlin had discovered an ss man who turned out to have been one of Hitler's bodyguards. Moreover, this man, Harry Mengershausen, claimed to have seen where Hitler and Braun had been burned and buried. Apparently, he was reluctant to show the Russians at first, but was eventually persuaded to do so. He then led them to exactly "the same crater in which Ivan Churakov had discovered the bodies." In Mengershausen's subsequent testimony, he said that it had been his duty, between 20 and 30 April, to patrol the area of the New Chancellery between Hitler's study and the blue dining room (known to others as the Hall of Mosaics). It was from there, he said, that he had seen Günsche and Linge carry the bodies of Hitler and Eva Braun from the emergency exit of the Bunker into the open. "This aroused his interest and he watched carefully to see how things developed."

"Hitler's personal Adjutant Günsche poured gasoline over the bodies and ignited them. After half an hour the bodies of Hitler and his wife were consumed; they were taken to a crater at about one metre's distance from the above-mentioned emergency exit, and there buried." Mengershausen, who said he witnessed all this from a distance of about 600 metres, testified that he also saw Hitler's dog buried in the same crater on 29 April. The animal was an Alsatian with long ears, a black back and light flanks.

Continuing to quote Klimenko, Bezymenski wrote that the bodies of Hitler and Eva Braun and the two dogs were wrapped in blankets, put in wooden boxes (these turned out to be ammunition crates) and carried out of the Chancellery early on 5 May. They were taken to the Counter Intelligence premises of the 3rd Shock Army, in the Buch suburb of Berlin.

The first medical man to examine the remains was Dr Faust Shkaravski, a forensic physician who was at the time Chief Expert of Forensic Medicine with the First Belorussian Front. Shkaravski was half Ukrainian and half Polish who by that time had performed about a thousand autopsies. That same day Shkaravski attended a small house in the grounds of a commandeered clinic in Buch. He found nine corpses laid out in an unfurnished room. Later, he was joined by four other medical experts. The actual dissection of the corpses which were presumed to be of Hitler and Braun was made on 8 May.

Bezymenski summarised the findings of the autopsy. The work was simplest with General Krebs and the Goebbels children, since their bodies were not damaged by burning. "With Krebs, as with the six children, the experts detected at the incision of the chest and abdominal cavities 'a marked smell of bitter almonds'; the chemical tests of the internal organs established in each case the presence of cyanide compounds." Forensic scientists – and detective story fans – the world over know that the smell of bitter almonds, released when dissecting a body, indicates death by cyanide poisoning.

The corpses of Josef and Magda Goebbels were badly damaged by burning. However, between the teeth of Josef's lower jaw, a splinter of thin colourless glass, belonging to an ampoule, was found. Dissection of the lungs released "a faint smell of bitter almonds" and subsequent chemical analysis established the presence of cyanide in the blood and internal organs. With Magda Goebbels' corpse, "splinters from a thin-walled ampoule with a blue tip" were also found. Chemical analysis again established the presence of cyanide compounds.

This was important scientific evidence, for according to earlier accounts in the West, Magda and Josef Goebbels had been shot. This is something to which we shall return.

Next, they turned to the dogs. In the case of the Alsatian, splinters of a thin-walled glass ampoule were found both on the tongue and in the mucous membrane of the creature's muzzle. Analysis established the presence of cyanide compounds. The other dog, a smaller black creature, had been shot through the head. There were no glass fragments in the mouth of this animal but cyanide compounds were found in its body. It was concluded that: "Death was caused by poisoning with cyanide compounds and by a lethal head injury with extensive destruction of brain matter."

Bezymenski asked one of the foremost Soviet forensic experts, Professor Dr Vladimir Mikhailovitch Smolyaninov, what he made of the dogs. He replied: "You know, this looks very much like a so-called 'toxilogical test.' In the case of the one dog, the ampoule had been crushed in its mouth. The other dog had to swallow the ampoule and was then shot – with a shot from above, as can be seen from the report." Günsche later confirmed that just such a test had been carried out, and that Hitler had taken a keen interest in the results. Professor Haase had performed the poisoning.

Bezymenski then moved on to the remaining corpses in the Buch autopsy room. The examination concluded that the male corpse, disfigured by fire, belonged to a man whose height would have been 165 cm; he was aged between fifty and sixty, though in view of the damage it was very difficult to gauge this accurately. The right shinbone measured 39 cm and part of the cranium was missing. Regarding the skull, parts of the occipital bone, the left temporal bone, the lower cheekbones and the upper and lower jaws were preserved. The remains of the head were more severely burned on the right side of the cranium than on the left. Part of the brain could be seen but the corpse was completely lacking skin – just the remnants of charred muscles were found. The tongue was charred, "its tip is firmly locked between the teeth of the upper and lower jaws."

The report devoted quite a lot of detail to the teeth. In the upper jaw there were nine teeth connected by a bridge of yellow metal (gold). The lower jawbone, said the report, lay loose in the singed oral cavity. This jaw consisted of fifteen teeth, ten of which were artificial. Splinters of glass, part of an ampoule, were found in the mouth.

Some of the internal organs were examined and then the report continued, "The genital member is scorched. In the scrotum, which is singed but preserved, only the right testicle was found. The left testicle could not be found in the inguinal canal." The left foot of the corpse was also missing.

The Russians had by this time traced Frau Käthe Heusermann, the dental nurse who had assisted Dr Blaschke, the Führer's dentist. She had described Hitler's teeth in detail and confirmed that she had actually held in her hands the bridgework that had been found on the corpse. According to the Russians, her description of the teeth (including crowns and fillings) fitted exactly.

In its conclusions, the commission said that the trace of glass splinters in the oral cavity, and the smell of bitter almonds emanating from the bodies, permitted a conclusion "that death in this instance was caused by poisoning with cyanide compounds."

This was the totally unexpected bombshell. Hitler had not shot himself, as had been thought for the past twenty-three years. He had not died like a man, like a soldier, as Trevor-Roper had concluded. Instead, Hitler had taken the easy way out, the coward's way and had poisoned himself. Part of the skull was missing but there was no trace of a bullet wound in what was left of his remains. Bezymenski's account of the Russian commission's report therefore turned Trevor-Roper's findings on their head. If the forensic evidence could be believed, it seemed to settle matters once and for all. The world had to adjust in its ideas about Hitler's death.

Next, the commission turned to the female corpse. Once again charring made positive identification impossible but the commission concluded that the corpse came from a female aged between thirty and forty (Eva Braun had turned thirty-three in April 1945) and about 150 cm high. A gold bridge of the lower jaw was found on this corpse, showing four front teeth. Remnants of a glass ampoule were found in the oral cavity, but there were other signs of damage, too, namely traces of a splinter injury to the thorax and hemothorax, injuries to one lung and to the pericardium, where six small metal fragments were also found. The commission concluded that only shell splinters could have caused the injuries and the haemorrhage in the lungs.

Notwithstanding this, however, the commission concluded that the woman had died – like the man beside her – from poisoning by cyanide compounds.

Bezymenski described in detail how Käthe Heusermann had been traced. (This too is important for later.) She helped them locate Hitler's dental records, the x-rays of his teeth, which were located in Blaschke's office, the Führer's dentist. She also directed them to Fritz Echtmann, the dental technician who had actually made the bridges to Blaschke's specification. Bezymenski reported that both Heusermann and Echtmann confirmed that the bridges found on the corpses – and the jawbone itself – belonged to Hitler. Although the upper bridgework consisted only of gold, with no organic matter, Heusermann agreed that the gold showed traces where the bridge had been sawn through by Blaschke in October 1944 when extracting Hitler's sixth tooth.

All this seemed fairly conclusive but there was one other matter that Bezymenski addressed in detail: the fact that the male corpse presumed to be Hitler's had only one testicle. "This congenital defect had not been mentioned anywhere in the existing literature. But Professor Karl von Hasselbach, one of Hitler's physicians, remembers that the Führer always refused categorically to have a medical check-up. It is conceivable that this refusal was motivated by this physical abnormality."

Having considered the forensic material, Bezymenski then turned his attention to the human toll of the last days in the Bunker. In particular, he turned his eye to the mystery of the tragic deaths of the Goebbels children.

Bezymenski concentrated his attention first on Dr Helmut Kunz, another dentist who had treated Magda Goebbels in the past. Kunz said that on 27 April 1945 he had met Frau Goebbels in the hallway at the entrance to Hitler's bunker after dinner, between 8 and 9 pm. "She told me she wanted to speak to me about a highly important matter and added that the situation had reached the point where we would probably have to die. She therefore asked me to help her kill her children. I agreed.

"After this conversation Frau Goebbels led me to the children's bedroom and showed me all her children. The children were preparing to go to bed, and I did not speak to any of them."

Four days later, Kunz said Magda telephoned him between 4 and 5 pm. "She said that time was running out and asked me to come immediately to her bunker." He went but did not take any drugs with him. When he arrived, Goebbels was discussing something with Naumann, his deputy, and Kunz was forced to wait for ten minutes. When he was finally admitted, he was told that the Führer had died already and that later that night there was to be a mass break-out from the bunker. Magda wasn't leaving, however: she was determined to die and the children with her.

Kunz said that he suggested the children be put in care of the Red Cross but Magda wouldn't hear of it. Then Goebbels himself came back in and asked Kunz if he would help Magda "put the children to sleep." Kunz urged the Red Cross alternative a second time but was turned down once more. "After all," said the Minister of Propaganda, "they are the children of Goebbels!" Goebbels left the room. Kunz stayed but, for about an hour, Magda turned to her playing cards. Goebbels returned, this time with Schacht, his deputy Gauleiter of Berlin. He gave Schacht a pair of spectacles that had belonged to Hitler as a memento. Then Schacht left.

Goebbels now said they had to act quickly. Kunz and Magda walked through to the Goebbels bunker apartment although, on the way there, Kunz said, Magda took a syringe and filled it with morphine from the cabinet. She passed this syringe to him. When they entered the children's bedroom, Helga, Hilde, Helmut and the others were already in bed but not yet asleep.

Kunz's account continued: "Frau Goebbels said to the children: 'Children, don't be afraid, the doctor is going to give you an injection, a kind that is now given to all children and soldiers.' With these words she left the room. I stayed behind by myself and injected the morphine, beginning with the two older girls and then going on to the boy and the other girls." Kunz says he gave each child about 0.5 cc of morphine and that the exercise took him eight to ten minutes. When he was finished, he went back to the hall, where Magda was waiting, and told her they would have to wait another ten minutes for the morphine to take effect.

"After ten minutes Frau Goebbels went with me into the children's bedroom, where she stayed about five minutes placing in the mouth of each child a crushed ampoule containing potassium cyanide . . . As we returned to the hall, she said: 'This is the end'."

They both went to Goebbels' study, where Magda told her husband, "It's over with the children, now we have to think of ourselves." Goebbels said they had to hurry but Magda didn't want to die in the Bunker. Josef suggested the garden, but she said she preferred the idea of the Propaganda Ministry where he had worked all his life. Kunz then left, having been thanked by Goebbels for his help. He returned to his hospital.

This all seemed clear enough but the Russians soon received evidence that Kunz wasn't telling the truth. They had learned that Dr Stumpfegger, one of Hitler's doctors, had helped Kunz kill the Goebbels children. Kunz was therefore brought back for more questioning. This time he admitted right away that Stumpfegger had helped him. He said that after he had given morphine to the children and had waited with Frau Gobbels for the drug to take effect, he had lost his nerve and was unable to offer any more help to Magda when she asked him. Instead, he found Stumpfegger, who was sitting in the dining room of the Führerbunker, and brought him back to the hall outside the children's bedroom. However, Magda Goebbels was no longer there. "Stumpfegger immediately went into the bedroom. I waited next door. Four or five minutes later Stumpfegger came back with Frau Goebbels from the children's bedroom; he left immediately without saying a word to me. Frau Goebbels did not speak either, she only wept."

When asked why he had made no reference to Stumpfegger's presence before, Kunz said that he had been so shocked that he had simply forgotten about the other doctor's involvement. This was scarcely credible but the Soviets appeared to accept it.

Bezymenski continued that the corpses had been burned completely after the autopsies and their ashes "strewn to the wind". He then tackled the issue as to why the Soviet results had not been published earlier. "Not because of doubts as to the credibility of the experts," he felt constrained to admit. "By the end of May their conclusions were submitted to the highest command of the state and army, which recognised the medical examination as final." He added: "There is no doubt that Y. V. Stalin showed considerable interest in the fate of Hitler. [Marshal] G. K. Zhukov remembers that Stalin frequently inquired about him and indicated that investigations should be continued . . .

Was Y. V. Stalin so sceptical because he did not wish to accept that Hitler had 'escaped' his just punishment? Those who were involved in the investigation remember that other considerations played a far larger role. First, it was resolved not to publish the results of the forensic-medical report but to 'hold it in reserve' in case someone might try to slip into the role of 'the Führer saved by a miracle'.

Secondly, it was resolved to continue the investigations: "in order to exclude any possibility of error or deliberate deception."

So a new phase of investigation was begun. This was the interrogation of a great many people who had lived in the Bunker to see if Hitler "would have been physically able" to flee Berlin in the last days of April 1945. The Russians drew up a list of all the people who had managed just such a feat, including: Hanna Reitsch, Artur Axmann, Walter Naumann, Bormann, Willi Müller, Himmler, Erich Koch (who continued to evade capture in West Germany, as it then was, until 1950).

Against this background the testimony of Mohnke, Rattenhuber, Günsche and Baur became even more important. Although he had been captured, at this point Linge had not been apprehended by the Soviet forces investigating Hitler's death. He had tried to blend in with the mass of prisoners of war, hoping to go unnoticed. However, he had about him one compromising object – a watch inscribed with Hitler's name. He gave this watch to a woman, a perfect stranger who was standing by the roadside as the prisoners were led through the streets of Berlin. He miscalculated. The woman spotted Hitler's name immediately and reported the watch to the Russian military authorities. It did not take them long to run Linge to earth.

The valet was then subject to intensive interrogation, as a result of which the Russians concluded that Hitler was perfectly capable of leaving Berlin up until 28 April, but that he had refused to follow the advice he was receiving on all sides. "But Hitler's physical disintegration and his demoralisation had advanced to such a point that he could no longer contemplate leaving the bunker. After 20 April he no longer dared venture into daylight and the explosions of the Russian shells made him shudder."

The Russians therefore concluded that Hitler did not leave Berlin but remained in the Bunker and committed suicide. The only question which remained was the method he had chosen. According to their own autopsy report of the cadaver in the crater he had taken cyanide, yet many reports published in the West said that he had shot himself. Which was correct?

"Little by little," Bezymenski wrote, "the news came through that Hitler had shot himself. This version had maintained itself in various memoirs and also in numerous historical research works." But he drew attention to the fact that the testimony of Günsche and Linge concerning Hitler's suicide had contained "curious ambiguities", ambiguities which had not been cleared up even after their release from custody. He pointed out that Linge had told *Der Spiegel* that Hitler had shot himself in the left temple using his left hand. But this was extremely unlikely, not only because the Führer was not left-handed but because his hands in any case shook very badly. The tremble in Hitler's left hand, said Bezymenski, was even worse than in his right.

He went on to note that Linge subsequently changed his testimony, to say that Hitler had shot himself with the right hand. This was too much. Bezymenski accordingly produced a table in which he showed that, by 1968, there had been no fewer than five accounts of Hitler's suicide which differed in some crucial details, such as where the bullet entered his body and where his body was in the death room in relation to Eva Braun's.

Bezymenski's conclusion was not that Hitler had escaped death, or anything sensational of that kind, but that his entourage had "purposely tried to hide the truth in order to foster the legend that the Führer had shot himself like a man."

He himself considered the idea of whether or not Hitler may have shot himself *and* taken poison. He dismissed out of hand the possibility that Hitler could have shot himself first and then taken the poison; that didn't make sense for obvious reasons. Next he considered the sequence the other way around. He concluded that it was "unlikely". Cyanide acts instantly, he said, and so this scenario was no more likely than the other. He confirmed his instinct by approaching the Soviet forensic scientist, Professor Dr Vladimir Mikhailovich Smolyaninov, to ask whether or not he had ever come across such a set of events. Smolyaninov said that in his entire career he had never encountered a single instance. Moreover, he said, such a method of suicide would have required a strong will, the ability to act quickly and a steady pair of hands. None of these attributes could be applied to Hitler in his last days.

Finally, Bezymenski's book entertained the possibility that Hitler may have taken poison but had then been shot by someone else. There was some indirect evidence for this, because of certain things Hitler was alleged to have said during his last days. A book published on Eva Braun in 1968 had referred to the testimony of four of Hitler's secretaries (Frau Wolf and Frau Schröder as well as Frau Junge and Frau Christian). They remembered that Hitler had said – when discussing armed resistance as the Russians were closing in on Berlin and he was considering whether he personally should fight to the last alongside his troops – that: "I can no longer hold a rifle, I would break down in the first hours, and who would then give me the *coup de grâce?*"

On 29 April, another significant exchange was supposed to have taken place between Krebs and Hitler. Once again suicide was the subject of discussion.

"The best way," said Krebs, "would be to shoot oneself in the mouth."

"Of course," Hitler replied, "but who would finish me off if my wound wasn't mortal? And I could never bring myself to shoot Eva."

Bezymenski then considered each of the men around Hitler, to see who might have delivered the *coup de grâce*. Bormann, he thought, was too cowardly. Moreover, he was a man who still hoped to rescue the Third Reich and was eager to play a major role. He would not have jeopardised his position with such a controversial act. Baur, Bezymenski said, was too busy hiding the painting of Frederick the Great that Hitler had given him as a farewell gift. He simply wasn't on hand.

Mohnke didn't appear to know that Hitler had been shot. He said he had been told as early as 30 April about Hitler's "self-poisoning". Rattenhuber, on the other hand, said that he had entered the bunker at about 4 pm on 30 April when Linge told him that the Führer had committed suicide and that he – Linge – "had executed the most difficult order in his life." Rattenhuber already claimed he knew that Linge had obtained potassium cyanide from Stumpfegger for Hitler and his wife. Rattenhuber said he had been shocked by Linge's words and, although Hitler "had taken his leave" of him, found it necessary to sit down, the shock was so great. Linge had outlined to Rattenhuber what had subsequently happened – how the bodies had been wrapped in blankets and taken out to the garden – but Linge also mentioned that there had been blood on the carpet. "As I looked at him with astonishment, knowing that Hitler had taken potassium cyanide, he [Linge] told me that Hitler had ordered him to leave the room and re-enter it ten minutes later, once everything was quiet, and to execute his order. I told Linge that I knew what he meant about 'the most difficult order' when he placed Hitler's pistol on the table of the ante-chamber."

Rattenhuber added that he was not the only person in the Bunker who knew about Linge's "most difficult order". According to him, Kriminalkommissar Hoegl had also been told by Linge that he was to carry out such an order. "I came to the conclusion," said Rattenhuber, "that Hitler did not entirely trust the effect of the poison on his organism and therefore ordered his valet Linge to go into his room after a certain lapse of time and shoot him." Such a sequence was entirely possible, said Bezymenski, because "it is known that certain chemical substances (for instance, basic compounds) exert a neutralising effect on cyanide." He pointed to Rasputin, who did not react to cyanide "because he was an alcoholic". Bezymenski conceded that as Hitler had been taking an immense quantity of drugs during the last years of the war and he was thus right to assume that some of these might have neutralised the effects of the cyanide. That was one reason, perhaps, why he had insisted on a trial poisoning with his dog, Blondi.

Despite all this evidence and speculation, however, Bezymenski said that the Russians had at first come to believe that it was Günsche and not Linge who had delivered the *coup de grâce*. He didn't say why they took this view, adding only that the medical experts thought this all conjecture anyway. Both Smolyaninov and Shkaravski said that the fact of Hitler's poisoning was "incontrovertible". "No matter what is asserted today, our Commission could not detect any traces of gun shot on 8 May 1945. Hitler poisoned himself."

Bezymenski's report, coming on top of the change in testimony of Linge and Baur, threw the whole question of Hitler's death into disarray. Had Hugh Trevor-Roper been misled and, if so, had he been misled deliberately? If so, why? Was there some wide conspiracy to deliberately confuse the issue for political purposes?

And were the Russians themselves playing games? As Erich Kuby put it in *The Russians in Berlin*: "It was in the interests of the Führer's entourage that the idol of the Third Reich should end his life by shooting himself courageously with a gun. It was just as much in the interests of the Soviet side that Hitler should have poisoned himself like a coward. Both sides have weighty reasons to hide the truth." On this reasoning, a botched self-poisoning, with a servant administering the fatal shot, was the most demeaning end of all.

Despite the bombshell that Bezymenski's book delivered, it too threw up as many questions as it answered. The truth of Hitler's death was no closer to being settled.

4

1979: "HITLER WAS NOT A COWARD"

Now our detective search jumps forward a decade, to 1979.

James O'Donnell had been an American soldier in 1945, part of the US 2nd Armoured Division which had taken Magdeburg on the Elbe. Like other Allied soldiers he had been allowed into Berlin on 4 July. On that same day he made his descent into Hitler's Bunker. This sparked a long fascination with the building on his part, a fascination he believed that was shared by much else of humankind. O'Donnell said he was once told by the eminent psychoanalyst Dr Carl Gustav Jung, shortly before his death in 1961, that he believed the Berlin Bunker was: "a dark reflection of a universal symbol in the collective unconscious of our culture".

Jung's opinion clearly had a marked impact on O'Donnell because over the next few years he began work for a book devoted solely to life in the Bunker in the last days. In the course of his research he tracked down a great many people who had shared those last few weeks, including Hitler's valet Linge, his SS Adjutant Günsche, General Mohnke, the telephone operator Rochus Misch, Käthe Heusermann the dental nurse and several others. When *The Berlin Bunker* was published in 1979 it brought more details of the death of Hitler to light.

The part of O'Donnell's endeavours which interest us takes up the story at lunch on that last day, 30 April 1945, the lunch that Eva Braun did not attend. O'Donnell interviewed both the secretaries Gerda Christian and Gertrud Junge about those events. Gerda Christian recalled a remarkable number of details about the lunch. She said, for instance, that there was a conversation about the proper mating of dogs. There was another exchange about how French lipstick was made from grease collected from Paris sewers during the War. This meticulous detailed background fact-finding not only shows O'Donnell's thoroughness, but also illustrates how witnesses sometimes remember seemingly insignificant things at a later date. The wayward nature of the human memory is an important factor in our detective story.

Just after that last lunch, O'Donnell reported, Trudl Junge took it upon herself to visit Eva Braun in her private rooms. She found Braun sitting in front of her dresser, going through her things and preparing to make a number of gifts of quite valuable items. She had, apparently, already given two large bundles to her maid, Liesl Ostertag. Her mood, when Trudl Junge entered, was "almost exuberant" and she gave her a silver-fox fur wrap: "Trudl, sweetheart, here's a present for next winter and your life after the War. I wish you all the luck in the world. And when you put it on, always remember me and give my very best to our native Bavaria, *das schoene Bayern* [beautiful Bavaria]."

Only after this did Hitler and Braun make their last appearance in the main corridor of the bunker to say farewell. The ceremony lasted but a few minutes. "No one later recalled any immortal words," wrote O'Donnell. "In the awkward silence that followed it was finally Linge who, taking his cue from the Führer, opened the door leading to Hitler's private apartment." This was when Hitler turned to Linge and ordered him to join the break-out group and to serve "the man who will come after me". Hitler's last words in public were thus defiant, assuming that the Reich would live on.

Hitler had placed Linge in charge of events from this point. The valet was to wait ten minutes and then to enter the room if no sound had been heard. Trudl Junge recollected how Linge lost his composure at this stage. For no apparent reason, he ran wildly up the steep steps towards the emergency exit and out into the garden where he encountered heavy artillery gunfire raining down. Thereupon, he turned and hurtled back down the stairs. "All the others simply watched Linge's antics in amazement."

Günsche was more composed. He rounded up some bodyguards, who were posted in the upper level, ready to carry the bodies outside to be burned. Then he stationed himself outside the door to Hitler's private rooms "feet apart, clasping his pistol before his breast."

Everyone expected the Führer's death at any moment. All were listening hard for a gun shot, even two, that would signal the end. Günsche told O'Donnell that it did cross his mind they wouldn't hear anything, not only because the door to Hitler's quarters was a heavy, vault-like steel door, but also because there was in fact a second door beyond the anteroom, leading to Hitler's living room.

At this point O'Donnell was told something entirely new, something significant. It was very curious no one had mentioned it before. Apparently Magda Goebbels suddenly appeared. She had missed the leave-taking ceremony in the corridor and came running towards Günsche. "Surprised and perplexed, Günsche flourished his pistol and tried to wave her back. But she was so frantic and so determined to see Hitler that Günsche relented." He opened the vault-like door and entered the anteroom to relay Frau Goebbels' request. But this was Magda Goebbels, who had been in love with Hitler down the years and she wouldn't wait. She pushed past Günsche and "lunged" into Hitler's study. The intrusion lasted for two or three minutes but Hitler wouldn't be swayed by the emotional Magda, who was still certain he had the chance to get away and head south. Magda left the Führer's quarters and, "sobbing and trembling", walked back past the others and returned to her own quarters. She didn't even acknowledge her husband.

This episode, coming just after Linge's wild antics, must have been very unnerving for all the others present, adding to the unreality of the situation. But there was more to come – in the shape of Artur Axmann, head of the Hitler Youth. He had arrived from his battle station across Wilhelmplatz, accompanied by Major Günther Weltzin, his senior aide. "Both wore wet handkerchiefs, tied bandit-style over their faces, to protect their eyes from hot ash and phosphorous fumes." Axmann also wanted to see Hitler, and approached Günsche. But this time the adjutant was firm. "Too late," he said. "Too late for anyone."

According to Trevor-Roper's account, it was shortly after this that a single shot was heard by those standing outside the "vault-like steel door." But given his account was based chiefly on the testimony of Hitler's driver, Erich Kempka – who wasn't even there at the crucial moment – O'Donnell was now able to state that Kempka had: "sheepishly admitted to me in 1974, he was not even among those present in the corridor. He was en route to the bunker from the chancellery – and was thus above ground at the time."

O'Donnell had done his best to get a consistent story from the eyewitnesses he had tracked down. Axmann, for instance, said: "Nobody was standing closer to that door than I, that is for sure. I have very good ears, and I was listening intently. The 1945 testimony of both Linge and Kempka just does not stand up; they must have been confused or were under interrogation pressure. Linge, for example, was really beside himself, running up and down those stairs like that."

The ss Adjutant Günsche was also frank with O'Donnell, or as frank as he would ever be. It was his opinion – or so he said – that the Russians were suspicious that either he himself or someone else very close to Hitler had actually shot the Führer. He said that in Moscow he was asked to sign a protocol to the effect that Hitler did not shoot himself. He refused. He did say that there were six people close to the outer door – Goebbels, Linge, Bormann, Krebs, Burgdorf, Axmann. "None of us heard a shot. I believe this was because of the sealed double doors. Both these doors were fireproof, gasproof, hence sound-proof." O'Donnell sent Günsche's evidence to Kempka, who now corroborated it. Kempka now admitted that he had told British and American interrogators that he had heard a shot because: "it seemed to be what they had wanted to hear." In truth, he had not heard any-thing of the sort.

O'Donnell regarded Axmann and Günsche as the more reliable of the so-called eyewitnesses. He also paid particular attention to an account that Professor Haase had given to Professor Ernst-Günther Schenck, another doctor and ardent Nazi, less than half an hour after Hitler's death. Schenck said Haase told him that, some time between 3 and 4 am on 30 April – hours before he had died – Hitler had once again questioned Haase on the pistol-and-poison method he had recommended earlier on.

Using this testimony – and bearing in mind what Axmann and Günsche said – O'Donnell now outlined a set of events which he re-garded as "a fair reconstruction of what most probably happened." He said that Hitler had in his possession two pistols, a Walther 7.65 calibre and a Walther 6.35 calibre. The larger gun he had carried with him for about a week. He had been observed removing it from his bed-room safe by Julius Schaub, a senior Adjutant. The smaller gun he had worn for many years, concealed in a leather holster sewn inside his trousers. At the critical moment, O'Donnell said, the smaller gun was placed on the table in front of Hitler – presumably as a precaution, in case the larger gun should jam.

Hitler and Eva sat on the narrow blue and white sofa. Eva had taken off her buckskin pumps and had tucked her feet under her body. Eva too had a Walther 6.35 calibre pistol and they both put them on a small round table in front of them. Both had poison vials and each put one vial on the table near the guns – Hitler's was placed between his gun and a vase; Eva's was between her gun and a raspberry coloured silk scarf. They both put the second vial in their mouth.

Hitler had told Haase – who repeated it to Schenck and through him to O'Donnell – that "we both want to go together when we go". Haase also said that, after his last conference with Hitler in the early hours of 30 April, he had visited Eva Braun and told her "simply bite quickly into your capsule the moment you hear a shot." O'Donnell concluded: "She apparently did just that, having some reason to fear that the sight of her dead lover might shatter her resolution. Eva Hitler was thus the only person to hear the single shot that many millions would have been delighted to hear."

O'Donnell was convinced that Hitler placed his black Walther directly to his right temple, "right-angled at eyebrow level," then squeezed the trigger as he simultaneously bit into his capsule. "Given his physical condition, this clearly called for one last, vehement act of concentrated will power ... The smoking pistol slipped from Hitler's right hand and fell to the carpet at his feet – a sign that the poison, potassium cyanide, had done its job quickly, for most people who commit suicide with pistols are usually found clutching the weapon tightly."

O'Donnell had been told that Linge was the first to go in, after ten minutes. When Linge opened the door the strong fumes, from the pistol and cyanide, made his eyes smart and, again, his nerve failed. He closed the door and went back for the others. This second time Bormann led the way, followed by Linge, Günsche, Goebbels and Axmann. O'Donnell claimed what happened next was agreed to by all three surviving witnesses he'd questioned, Günsche, Linge and Axmann.

Eva Hitler's body had hardly moved, her feet were still tucked up under her body. Her pistol was by her coloured scarf. Hitler had slumped over but he was still on the sofa. "Blood was oozing in steady drips from his right temple," wrote O'Donnell. The vase on the round table, filled only that morning with tulips and white narcissi, had fallen over, spilling water on Eva's blue chiffon dress. There was a stain near one of her thighs. The vase was on the floor but had not broken. Linge, still dazed, picked it up and examined it for cracks.

The others were dazed too. "At least two minutes – two very long minutes – passed before any of us said or did anything, except watch what Linge did with the white vase," according to Günsche.

Günsche finally pulled himself together and ordered Linge to move the chairs and table, so they could spread two woollen military blankets on the floor. He then left the death room to find some young officers who could help with the carrying. Just at that moment Dr Ludwig Stumpfegger arrived. He examined the bodies and pronounced Hitler and Braun dead.

Next came the Head of Hitler's Bodyguards, Johann Rattenhuber, suffering from a hangover from the dance the night before. Rattenhuber was particularly stunned by the news of Hitler's death, so much so that he did not have the nerve to go and see the dead body for himself but simply slumped on a chair and started to moan and groan. He noticed that Linge had brought the two Walther 6.35s out of Hitler's suite. Not knowing that General Krebs and Professor Haase had recommended the poison-and-pistol method – and hearing Linge talk about a pool of blood on the rug near Hitler's end of the sofa – Rattenhuber assumed that the Führer had been given a *coup de grâce*, most likely by Linge or Günsche. He stuck to his story, O'Donnell said, even after he had been captured by the Russians.

O'Donnell explained that he'd seriously considered the possibility that Linge and Günsche were still lying. By the time he interviewed them in 1974 both men had become successful businessmen, Linge in Hamburg and Günsche across the river from Bonn. Nearly thirty years on, both remained staunch admirers of their former chief and "neither would want to be known as 'the man who shot the Führer'." But notwithstanding this, O'Donnell chose to believe them. The clinching matter, for him, was something that Schenck had said following his conversation with Haase. "Many people tend to forget that Adolf Hitler was not alone when he shot himself. He was in the presence of a brave woman who was very much in love with him. Why, therefore, should he arrange a *coup de grâce* for himself but not for her? One can despise Hitler, believe only the worst of him, if one will, but we should not diabolize him. The man was not a coward. Moreover, as we know him, he was a great actor and a born show-off, above all before women. For him to have flinched at this last moment, before Eva Braun, *that* would have been quite out of character."

Regarding the burning and burial of the bodies. O'Donnell came up with yet another new witness to add to the guards Erich Mansfeld, Hermann Karnau and the bodyguard, Harry Mengershausen. This was Sergeant Hilco Poppen who was on patrol near the Old Mosaic Room of the Reichschancellery and about 150 metres from the Bunker. (Mengershausen was some 600 metres away.) Poppen saw the procession. "The bodies of the two Hitlers," he reports, "were still wrapped in blankets. With his binoculars, he could just make out the face of Eva Braun; he had no idea, of course, who she was." By the time he was making his statement to O'Donnell, Poppen knew that Hitler and Braun had married. At the time, however, Braun had long been kept in the background. It was therefore not so surprising that he did not recognise her. Poppen also observed three ss officers lower the bodies into a shallow ditch "less than ten metres from the Bunker exit". Otherwise, his evidence corroborated Mansfeld's, Mengers-hausen's and Karnau's.

Throughout that day and night, a succession of people were sent up into the garden to report on what was happening to the cadavers. O'Donnell felt that these reports claiming that the bodies were now no more than ash were exaggerated. Following Hitler's death it was noticeable in the bunker that the mood had changed. A selection of jazz and swing music was played from a loudspeaker in the canteen, the lower ranks no longer saluted the officers. Very few people, O'Donnell suggested, took much interest in the corpses, perhaps to the degree that those who were sent to see what was happening to them may not have given them due care and attention. What's more, the Russians were still shelling the Reichschancellery. But O'Donnell did add one gruesome fact which was to prove contentious later. According to Linge, who may either have seen this for himself – or else got it from one of the other soldiers – "Eva Braun's once-trim figure had jack-knifed, under *rigor mortis*, into what the morticians call an 'eques-trian posture'; that is, she was now sitting upright as if riding in a saddle. Both arms were outstretched and her hands seemed to be holding imaginary reins."

O'Donnell's account of the burial of the bodies was very similar to Trevor-Roper's, with one interesting addition. One of the soldiers who was burying the bodies in the crater came back to the bunker and asked "with a certain sense of awe and even dignity" for a flag. One could not be found, not even a swastika banner.

O'Donnell now turned his attention to Goebbels and, like Bezymenski before him in *The Death of Adolf Hitler*, focused on the Goebbels chil-dren. "In my interviews with even the most hard-boiled Bunker survivors," he wrote, "I found no theme quite so hushed up as the fate of the six Goebbels children. The oldest was Helga (aged twelve), her father's favourite. Intelligent, tall, mature for her age; she had her father's walnut eyes and dark hair; then came Hilde (eleven), the prettiest, also a brunette; Helmut (ten), the only boy, a dreamy youngster with bad grades in school; Holde (eight), blonde, the *Familiendepp*, the one the others always teased; Hedde (six), blonde; Heidi (not yet five), the family pet." Life for them was a strange upside-down world and not unexciting. Their company no doubt provided a welcome change for many of the people cooped up in the Bunker.

O'Donnell reports that there were several plans to "whisk" them away from the Bunker. Both Albert Speer (architect and once Minister for Armaments) and Werner Naumann (one of Goebbels' senior aides) had worked out their own plans and Brigadeführer Mohnke had even agreed to put a tank at their disposal. Eva Braun's maid had a soft spot for Heidi and was willing to take her with her on the break-out. But their parents were determined that their children would die with them.

Magda Goebbels was in many ways no less charismatic than her husband. O'Donnell, too, found "witness after witness' prepared to attest that she had been obsessed with the Führer for many years. She herself admitted to friends, in letters, that she was in love with him. She kept her feelings hidden from Hitler but, as Kempka put it to O'Donnell, "whenever she was in the presence of the Führer, I could hear her ovaries rattling." She had a melodramatic nature and it was this, O'Donnell suggested, that led her to her "mammoth sacrifice".

O'Donnell reported that there was still disagreement as to what exactly had happened to the six children. Some of the people he talked to said that Stumpfegger had administered the poison, others that it was Magda Goebbels' dentist, Helmut Kunz. Kunz refused to talk to O'Donnell or to anyone else. He had been involved in a libel and slander suit in the mid 1960s, when he had denied under oath that he had given the Goebbels children any lethal injections. This action had arisen out of the Bezymenski book and because fellow prisoners in the Soviet Union had testified that he had first admitted culpability, only to subsequently deny the charge.

O'Donnell's conclusion was that Magda Goebbels had killed her children herself. The evidence, he said, was quite damming. First, Frau Goebbels had written a letter to Harald Quandt, her son by an earlier marriage. This letter was one of those taken out of the Bunker at the last minute by Hanna Reitsch. In it Magda Goebbels had written: "God will forgive me as a mother provided I have courage to carry out this deed myself and do not leave it to others. When the time comes, I shall give my darlings sleeping potions and then poison, a soft and painless death." The second piece of evidence was a statement by

Goebbels' aide, Naumann. He said he had tried to talk Magda out of it, but had failed. He said there were no eyewitnesses but that doctors Stumpfegger and Kunz were standing in an adjoining room. Naumann said that Magda had gathered her children all in one room and told them that they would all be leaving shortly for Berchtesgaden with "Uncle Führer". Putting each child to bed, she gave them chocolates "to prevent air sickness". The chocolate was infused with a soporific drug called Finodin. They never woke from this "sleep".

The third piece of evidence that led O'Donnell to his conclusion came from Rochus Misch, the telephone operator. At about 2 pm on the afternoon of 1 May, he saw the three younger Goebbels children – Holde, Hedde and Heidi – playing with a ball in the Bunker. Hitler was already dead and that part of the Bunker was quiet. Misch gave the children some soda, he says. Later they disappeared, only to reappear around 5 o'clock, followed by Helga, Hilde, Helmut and their mother, who was wearing a long-skirted navy-blue dress with white collar, cuffs and piping. "Her face," Misch recollected, "was ashen." She led her six children into a room opposite Misch, the same room as where Frau Junge typed out Hitler's Will and Political Testament.

For a while Misch watched as Magda combed the children's hair. They were all dressed in white nightgowns. Everyone kept peculiar hours in the Bunker and this was apparently their normal bedtime. The five younger children chatted quietly. Twelve-year-old Helga suspected something, Misch felt, for she was sobbing softly. Then, after a while, and without speaking to Misch, Magda led the children, "like a duck with six ducklings" up the spiral staircase back to the upper bunker. "Heidi, the youngest and a little flirt, turned back to the sergeant and said, '*Misch, Misch, du bist ein Fisch*' ('Misch, Misch, you're a fish'). She was giggling. But her sister, Helga, was dragging her feet, and Magda Goebbels had to push her on her way."

About half an hour later, Misch remembered Werner Naumann appearing and reporting that Stumpfegger was giving the Goebbels children "some doped candy". The parents had insisted that the children die now, because time was running out.

Another hour passed. Eventually Magda Goebbels reappeared. "There was no expression on her face. Her blue eyes were ringed with red. At first she stood there, just wringing her hands. Then she pulled herself together and lit a cigarette . . .There was a small champagne bottle, a *piccolo*, which someone had left on the long table in the main corridor. She took it and proceeded into the room next to the watch-room, the one Dr Goebbels had been using all week as his study. She had left this door open. I got up, walked past, and could see that she had taken out a pack of small cards and had begun to lay down a solitaire hand. Instinctively, I knew that her children were no more of this world."

It was Misch's belief that Magda's grim task did not go off without problems. He was sure that Helga woke in fright as her mother approached her bedside, undeceived by her mother's lie about the airplane ride: she therefore may not have swallowed the drugged chocolate. Another possibility was that for her, as the tallest and oldest, the dosage was insufficient. Either way, the Russian autopsy report, according to O'Donnell, reported that the corpse of the twelve-year-old showed "several black and blue bruises". The suspicion grew that she had been held down at one stage or another, against her wishes. This only added to the horror of the situation.

Misch's account outlined a weird scenario. After the killing of the children there was, he said, a sort of reminiscence meeting. Josef and Magda Goebbels were there, so was Werner Naumann, Hitler's pilot Hans Baur, Walter Hewel and General Krebs. It was 6.30 pm. Goebbels greeted Misch when he arrived and then sank back into his chair, recalling the early days of Nazism, the heady days between 1928 and 1933 when *Horst Wessel* marching songs had inspired them. He was vitriolic about the Jews and money changers. He did not speak of his family. "Magda Goebbels just sat there, saying little, head high. She was chain-smoking and sipping champagne. I did not ask about the children because someone, either Baur or Hewel, had whispered to me that they were already dead."

Misch added an extraordinary fact, given these were the last days of the War. Throughout that day – 1 May – a week before the unconditional surrender, there were only about three or four calls *into* the Bunker. Contact with military headquarters at Zossen was minimal.

At 8.15 that evening, Goebbels went to his wife's room. They then descended to the lower bunker where they met General Mohnke, Captain Schwaegermann and Olds, his junior aide. All of them knew what was coming, O'Donnell said. Mohnke then took up the story. "Going over to the coat rack in the small room that had served as his study [Goebbels] donned his hat, his scarf, his long uniform overcoat. Slowly, he drew on his kid gloves, making each finger snug. Then, like a cavalier, he offered his right arm to his wife. They were wordless now. So were we three spectators. Slowly but steadily, leaning a bit on each other, they headed up the stairs to the courtyard."

It was now 8.30 pm, the time of the black-out. At the foot of the stairs to the emergency exit, they passed six jerry cans "standing ready". At the top of the stairs was an SS officer, also standing ready, in case help was needed.

It was not. Earlier versions of this part of the story had an SS officer firing the shots which killed Josef and Magda Goebbels. According to O'Donnell's evidence, however, they had rehearsed very carefully Professor Haase's preferred method – poison first, immediately followed by gunshot before the poison took effect. "Magda went first. She bit into her capsule, sank slowly to the soft spring earth. She was wearing, for a brooch, Adolf Hitler's golden party badge, which the Führer had given her as a parting present the day before his own death. Her husband fired a bullet into the back of her blonde head. Goebbels then bit into his own capsule, squeezed the trigger of his Walther P-38 pistol, and put a bullet through his right temple." The SS officer called to Schwaegermann and together they set fire to the bodies. As the Russians discovered only hours later, they botched that.

5

THE DISCOVERY OF HITLER'S SKULL

So, to recapitulate, there had been at least three "authoritative" books about the death of Hitler by 1979, two by Western authors, one by a Russian, not to mention the many, many more articles and features which have not been reported here. One investigation had concluded that Hitler had died after he had shot himself in the mouth, a second that he had poisoned himself by cyanide, and a third that he had both poisoned himself *and* shot himself at one and the same time – in the temple, not the mouth. It was hardly an ideal situation.

Sightings of Hitler had dropped away – though a Canadian newspaper "reported" as late as 1992 that he had "died" in Latin America – and at one level this had now become an academic debate. But on another level there was a more serious issue. There is no question but that, for many people, the Nazi movement in general – and Hitler's personage in particular – had become synonymous with "evil". Remember Dr Jung's statement, mentioned in the last chapter? As such, there was an inexhaustible fascination with the Führer and with the manner of his ending. There was another issue, too, more subtle and perhaps more political. Over the years poisoning had come to be regarded as a "coward's" form of suicide, whereas shooting was considered to be more courageous, more dignified, more befitting a soldier and a head of state. The search for Hitler's way of dying was a search for his ultimate character.

We shall come back to this but for now we need to explore something else. It will be remembered that Lev Bezymenski had been given special access to the Russian records in 1968 which showed – as he believed – that a secret Soviet commission had looked into the death of Hitler in May 1945. It had reported back to Minister of the Interior, Lavrenti Beria and, via Beria, to Stalin. The Commission's conclusion was unequivocal: Hitler had poisoned himself. It will also be remembered that there were, according to Bezymenski, a number of reasons for not publicising these results, not least among them the need to keep something "in reserve" in case someone appeared as Hitler, claiming to have been miraculously saved from the Russian siege of Berlin and attempting to promote a neo-Nazi movement.

This had not been entirely convincing as an explanation for the lack of candour, even in 1968. By then twenty-three years had elapsed since the end of World War Two. If someone who were to lead a Nazi revival were to have claimed that he had miraculously escaped from the siege of Berlin, he might have been expected to have made his move well before then.

O'Donnell's book in 1979, eleven years after Bezymenki's, was fascinating. He was to be commended for all the new material he unearthed on what was thought to be well-trodden ground. But his book still did not settle the matter of Hitler's death. There were now three versions, all different: poison, shooting or poison and shooting. Readers could take their pick.

We now jump forward to the summer of 1992, when Ada Petrova went to visit Anatoli Prokopenko. She was interested in making a programme on the death of Stalin. Intrigued about the sequence of events between his stroke in the Kremlin at the end of February 1953 and his death several days later, she hoped to find information in the State Special Trophy Archive of which Prokopenko was Director. Perestroika and glasnost had led to many archives in Russian becoming more accessible. She hoped to take advantage of that fact.

After Prokopenko dropped his bombshell – that Hitler's skull was "right here in Moscow" – she changed tack and put the Stalin inquiry on the back burner, as a fascination with Hitler's death took its place. Eventually, she found the Führer's skull in the State Archive of the Russian Federation, a grey, eight-storey building on Bolshaya Pirogovskaya Street that some say resembles a granary tower. This chapter tells that story.

Three years later we can now be sure that, for reasons best known to themselves, the Russian authorities kept Lev Bezymenski in the dark. He was, quite simply, never given the full picture of what happened in the wake of the discovery of Hitler's and Eva Braun's corpses in the Reichschancellery crater. We can say this with certainty because we have been shown the *entire* Hitler Archive, six buff-coloured files of documents, plus charts and photographs mounted on blue board. Known as the Operation Myth file, its official number was 1-G-23. Its subtitle was "Hitler and his Entourage".

The documents in this file make it clear that there were several special *Sonderkommands* formed as the end of the War approached, each consisting of fifteen German-speakers. Their remit was to investigate the northern part of Germany, to search for documents and to confirm or deny rumours circulating in the Russian army that Hitler had escaped.

The files consist of copies of interrogation reports regarding the entourage who were held in Russia, internal Counter Intelligence memoranda and – most sensationally – details about a *second* Russian commission of inquiry which was not even referred to in passing by Bezymenski.

The documents show that about 800 people were interrogated and that roughly seventy members of Hitler's entourage were taken to Russia in 1945, including Hitler's dog handler, secretaries, chauffeur, signals and telegraph officers – anyone who could have been an eyewitness. After initial interrogation, they were dispatched into various camps. Ten of those closest to Hitler were transferred back from the camps to the Butyrka prison in Moscow on 16 February 1946. (There are three maximum security prisons in Moscow for "political" prisoners: the Lubjanka inner prison, Lefortovo and Butyrka.)

An order signed by Lieutenant-Colonel Amayak Kobulov, of the NKVD to the head of Butyrka, Colonel Alexander Pustynsky, directed that five separate prison cells be set aside for interrogation. Each cell was to accommodate two people, one prisoner and one "special officer" (that is, a stool pigeon, usually a German who'd agreed to collaborate): "special measures" were to be taken to "monitor the behaviour" of the inmates, presumably bugging devices. A special guard was to be mounted at all times. Baur, Linge, Misch, Günsche, Hentschel, Hans Hofbeck and others were transferred to the prison one by one. Every day, "operational material" was sent to Counter-Intelligence (Smersh) headquarters.

This operational material reports of direct interrogation – and what was told to the stool pigeons – provides fascinating reading for anyone interested in Hitler's death. For example, the reports show that Hitler's pilot Baur was a most unreliable witness. They also show why that may have been. One document notes that Baur – who had been wounded during the break-out and had had a leg amputated – was very afraid of physical punishment. "He said that he regretted the fact that he did not commit suicide [when he had the chance]. He asked for a pistol to shoot himself."

In the circumstances, Baur may well have told the Russians what he thought they wanted to hear. He certainly chopped and changed his story. At one time, he confessed to his stool pigeon – someone with the operational name of Hermann Hage – that he thought Hitler had deceived them all, that the preparations for the Führer's *escape* were "thorough and took a lot of time, so there would be no failure." He added that he thought Hitler's depression was an act, "that he just wanted to create an impression he had died – and had flown to Spain." Yet on another occasion Baur discussed with Hage Hitler's "dreadful death". On yet another occasion he agreed with the theory put forward by the telephone operator Rochus Misch that the "riddle" would never be uncovered and added that only one inmate of the prison knew everything, the Chief of Bodyguards, Rattenhuber. Then he said that the mystery of Hitler's escape was known only to two people – Rattenhuber and Hoegl, his deputy. Once when Hage expressed the view that Hitler wasn't dead, Baur replied, "well, I can't resurrect him." And on a fourth occasion, again in conversation with Hage in the cell, Baur gave still conflicting versions.

Rattenhuber's testimony – as revealed in the Myth file – was extensive and contains four particularly important pieces of information never published before. He said, first, that at about 9 am on 30 April, Eva Braun had left the Bunker and stood for some minutes in the garden of the Reichschancellery. As she returned, she'd said, "I wanted to look at the sun for the last time." The second important piece of information was that when Rattenhuber was slumped in the chair in the corridor outside Hitler's suite recovering from the shock, he claimed he could smell bitter almonds coming out of the death room. The third was that, during the last days, Hitler used to rail at Göring. "The fat pig!" Rattenhuber says he screamed, "the fat pig! He doesn't have enough courage to die with us!"

Rattenhuber's understanding was that some people had heard the shot and others had not: he didn't think this particularly unusual, given the bombardment going on above ground and the thickness of the door to Hitler's suite, which muffled sound.

Rattenhuber also said Hitler witnessed Blondi's death and that the dog did not die immediately, as has been said. Instead he "yelped out loudly and died after some convulsions, quivering. Hitler was definitely shocked when he saw the dog's rapid death and even here he made a 'Führer's' gesture."

Other documents in the Myth File report apparently vital testimony, but without attribution. For example, one paragraph says that certain witnesses believed that Hitler wasn't actually killed by cyanide, because he was a vegetarian – the idea being that the huge quantity of drugs he had been taking had neutralised the poison's effectiveness. These witnesses also claimed he was in enormous pain after he had taken the poison, crying and screaming. It was because of this that his Adjutant Günsche shot him in the mouth. Another unattributed paragraph records that Hitler was anxious to commit suicide before the Russians got too close because he feared they might infiltrate some sort of knock-out gas into the Bunker so he would be captured alive. A third paragraph records some witnesses testifying to the fact that Eva Braun's body had no bullet wounds and that, therefore, when "bullet wounds" were supposedly found in her lungs they doubted that this was her body. A fourth paragraph virtually turned the previous one on its head. These unidentified witnesses said that when Braun's body had been brought into the Reichschancellery garden it had been hit by shell splinters. Other unattributed documents pertaining to less important matters say that Eva Braun wrote to her sister on 23 April asking Gretl to hide her furs and all the bills from the Gaiser firm – though there is no indication as to why. Another document makes clear that the body of Hitler's double was buried in the courtyard of Lefortovo prison and that among the rumours picked up in the Reichschancellery in May 1945 was one that Hitler and Eva Braun had a twelve-year-old son. It all seemed conjecture more than evidence and The fact that the Russian interrogators did not attach names to some of these testimonies possibly means that they didn't believe what they were being told.

In the West, much has been made of the way Linge changed his testimony. The Myth File in Moscow contains two documents pertinent to Linge and his story. First, there is his interrogation report; second, there is the typescript of a book which he and Günsche were forced to write after the formal interrogations were over. The valet and the Adjutant were placed together in a cell and given extra privileges for their cooperation. Some of this information relates directly to the death of Hitler, other details just flesh out the man. What follows below is an amalgam, taken from both documents, selected to show what we regard as relevant when writing this book.

Linge admitted at one point that he thought "some" preparations had been made for Hitler's escape, but he may simply have been referring to plans (mentioned by Baur) to have a Condor aircraft on permanent standby in case the Führer changed his mind about fleeing south. Linge told the Russians that he and Martin Bormann did hear a shot. They entered the room. Hitler was on the left side of the settee dead. There was a blood stain at his right temple. (The Russian report adds here, in brackets, that according to British information Hitler had shot himself in the mouth.) On the floor, said Linge, there were two Walther pistols. Eva Braun was sitting on the right side, squatting, with her shoes on the floor. She, too, was dead. Linge claimed that no doctor was called, even though there were doctors in the Bunker. This conflicts with the testimony that Stumpfegger pronounced both corpses dead.

Linge also said that there were bloodstains on the wall of Hitler's living room, on the sofa and on the floor. There was a strong smell of almonds in the room. He added that Kempka fetched four canisters of petrol and that two were used in the burning of the bodies of Hitler and Braun.

Linge claimed to have inspected the corpses while they were burning in the Reichschancellery garden. No times were given in the documents, but Linge added that the bodies were badly burned, although still recognisable. The male corpse – Hitler's – had a bullet wound in the skull. The hole was the size of a kopek.

Linge also included the information that, in the last months, Hitler had felt that his signature was too elaborate (perhaps because of the tremor in his arms) and that therefore a rubber stamp had been produced. This detail is contained in a memorandum sent from Beria to Molotov; it seems to have crossed the Russians' minds that the signature on Hitler's Will and Political Testament may have been forged, using this stamp.

The book compiled by Linge and Günsche confirms that Hitler was very sentimental. He loved cats and dogs but, after he became Chancellor, his Scotch Terrier didn't suit his new style. He acquired his Alsatian, known as Blondi.

Hitler was very widely read, they claimed, and if he modelled himself on anyone it was the Roman Emperor Nero. He liked Nero's simplicity and believed that a human genius "should be conspicuous".

He got up between 11 am and noon and took a bath scented always with the essence of coniferous trees, such as pine.

Until 1943, he ate dinner with between sixteen and twenty people. He always ate vegetarian meals slightly heated-up because of his sore throat (inherited, he believed, from his father) and he always drank tepid rather than cold mineral water. He became vegetarian after he was poisoned in a gas attack in World War One. After that, he put himself on a strict diet though he loved sweets and herbal teas. He was very fond of poppy cake baked by his sister, Angela.

He was aware of the impact of his speeches and during them he became so agitated that his clothes were soaked in sweat. His face would become swollen and go red. Afterwards, he always went home, where he would rinse his throat with a throat medicine and drink a hot cup of tea with a shot of vodka in it. He would then take a hot bath and get into a warmed-up bath robe. These evenings always ended in the same way: only reminiscences were allowed, from the time of his struggle for power when he was rushing all over Germany, out-manoeuvring his rivals.

Linge and Günsche confirmed that, from the end of 1943, Hitler stopped dining at a big table, having become convinced that there was a traitor among his entourage. They also said that after the General's Plot in July 1944 – when he miraculously escaped death – Hitler acquired a nervous disease, with a strong tremor in his left hand.

Günsche's testimony – as made available to us for this book – also contained new material. At first, he had said that he did not think Hitler finally made up his mind to commit suicide until 29 April. He says that the Führer started worrying on that day because the Russian motorised units had reached the Anhalt railway station and Königsplatz and because the onslaught was beginning to affect the morale of the population. If this is true, it may have been this final twist of events which not only resolved Hitler to kill himself but also to marry Eva Braun.

Günsche's testimony also gives the names of the people he claimed had carried the corpses out of the Bunker – Hauptschahrführer Kruge, Obersturmführer Lindlofer and himself. He said he helped pull the corpse of the "Führer's wife" from the Bunker door. She was wrapped in a blanket but her head could be seen. And he further added that, when he returned to the Bunker, "the door to the Führer's personal suite was slightly ajar and a strong smell of almonds (potassium cyanide) was coming from there." This interrogation is dated 17 May 1945.

At this point we need to consider the importance of the second Russian commission. It is not altogether clear why a second commission was deemed necessary; though there are several possibilities. Obviously the first commission had many shortcomings and contradictions. For example, the autopsies of Adolf Hitler and Eva Braun did not include a dissection of the internal organs of either corpse. Therefore, the doctors could not say with scientific certainty that these organs contained cyanide compounds.

Another reason for the second commission were the continuing rumours from eyewitnesses, that Hitler may have escaped. Then there was Stalin's scepticism over Hitler's death. It is not known whether he considered the autopsy reports closely or whether he was simply obsessed with his former arch rival: while there was any chance that the Führer was still alive, he did not want to miss the opportunity of getting his hands on him.

A further reason was the power battle inside the Soviet hierarchy, between Smersh and the NKVD, the forerunner of the KGB. Smersh had made the running in the early days, and overseen the initial investigation and the autopsies. But the results were now seen as less than conclusive. If another organisation – the NKVD – carried out its own investigation and discovered new evidence, that would be a feather in its cap.

A final reason was a number of approaches from the Western Allies to the Russians. The Russians had doubts about their own autopsy reports, for reasons just given. Then on 31 October 1945 they were approached by Brigadier-General Brian Conrad, Head of US Intelligence. He said he had evidence that Hitler had died on 30 April at 2.30 pm and proposed a joint commission of the Britain, America and the Soviet Union to investigate the circumstances.

Lavrenti Beria, the most powerful security director in Soviet history, was inclined to assent to this request. But Abakumov, head of Smersh, was fiercely opposed as – apparently – was Stalin. Jealous that the Western Allies might have some evidence they lacked, however, the idea of a second commission began to look increasingly attractive to the Russians.

This took a while to organise, and there may have been additional and complicating factors in addition to those mentioned here. But, in April-May 1946, the second commission got under way. It was headed by the medical forensic specialist, Pyotr Semenovsky. In the USSR, Semenovsky was the most distinguished forensic expert of his day. He graduated from a German University and eventually became chief of the fingerprint department in the Moscow Bureau of Forensic Medical Examination, part of the Moscow Criminal Police.

Even this second commission was ambiguous, for the inquiry seems to have had two strands. In the first place, on 9 April 1946, Serov, then head of the NKVD, announced, in a letter to Kubulov, Minister of Internal Affairs, that a group of prisoners were to be sent to Berlin for the re-creation of the last days.

Although this was supposed to be a top-secret rendezvous, someone on the Russian side tipped off James O'Donnell, author of *The Berlin Bunker*, then working as a journalist for *Newsweek* and based in Berlin. Together with Marguerite Higgins of the New York *Herald Tribune*, who was paying the same tipster, he hurried across to the Bunker. "By now, the old emergency exit had become the only approach to the Bunker, although we knew the Russians were not allowing access to it. This time we were chased out into Wilhelmstrasse by four sullen sentries flourishing sub-machine guns. There we met a Russian officer who told us to vanish. He made his point with a drawn pistol.

"We vanished, but only around the corner into Vossstrasse, from which we sneaked into the New Reichschancellery, and climbed our way to the roof of that now-ghostly edifice. Two owls flitted by on noiseless wings. Our shaky rooftop perch was about 100 yards above and away from the Bunker and our view of the entrance was partly blocked. Dusk had now fallen. In the quiet we could hear voices and could make out the shadowy forms of some twenty people milling about the entrance. The action, to our disappointment, all seemed to be inside the Bunker. Those figures who did emerge outside were simply taking a cigarette break; we could see the orange glimmer. Half an hour passed, and as our eyes adjusted to the dark, we could see Russian uniforms, with the familiar soup-plate hats and baggy-rump trousers.

"Suddenly, lights illuminated the Bunker and the Old Chancellery garden. Now we could see cameramen and hear the whir of their cameras on what looked like a film set. Four or five Russian officers were giving directions to a group of about twelve actors clad in what seemed to be deep purple fatigue uniforms. A mélange of German words, Russian words, floated indistinctly across the chilly evening air. A scene was shot; we could hear the clapper. The performers filed back into the Bunker. The lights went out.

"But twenty minutes later, the same group emerged again to shoot a second scene. We guessed – correctly as it turned out – that the two scenes being played out must be the burial of the Hitlers and the suicides of Joseph and Magda Goebbels. As we already knew, these were the only two events that had taken place *outside* the bunker. Marguerite and I came to the conclusion that a Russian movie company was making a film documentary with Red Army help. Soon the whole mysterious troupe departed in trucks. An eerie event, we felt . . ."

Only later did O'Donnell find out that this was no mere film company but an actual reconstruction with the actual German personnel who had lived those last days in the Bunker in 1945. The "actors" – Günsche,

Linge, Baur, Rattenhuber and all the others – were returned to Moscow the very next day. They had spent less than twenty-four hours in Berlin.

The reconstruction was a good idea. Besides helping to build up an exact chronology of the last days, the Russian observers could also see how truthful the various witnesses were being. It was one thing for the prisoners to concoct a story, on which they might all agree in theory. But it was quite another for them to take the Russians through the events of the last days, in the Bunker itself. Any discrepancies would have immediately become apparent.

The records of Semenovsky's commission also show that Linge was taken back to the Bunker, alone, and led into Hitler's living room, where the suicide took place. There, he was instructed to verify the exact location of the desk, the round table, the sofa on which Hitler had shot himself and the rest of the furniture in the room. Various measurements were taken.

But this was only one strand of the inquiry. In the other, instituted on 16 May 1946, Pyotr Semenovsky was ordered to draw up a map of the Old and New Reichschancelleries and of the Bunker; to take photographs; to carry out an inspection of the walls, floor and ceilings; to search for traces of blood; to inspect the furniture; to thoroughly inspect the places where the corpses had initially been found; to look for personal belongings that might help these investigations; to carry out new autopsies; to obtain new forensic evidence of the corpses, including age, distinguishing marks, reasons of death; to take photographs and x-rays. This protocol was signed by Lieutenant-Colonel Klausen, deputy head of the operational department of the Chief Directorate of POWs and Internees of the USSR Ministry of Internal Affairs, Inspector in charge of Special Tasks, Military-Colonel Osipov and Semenovsky himself.

Visiting Berlin, the inquiry produced evidence as to the exact layout of the death room, and the surrounding area of the Bunker. Among other things, it verified that the stone staircase to the emergency exit was one metre wide, with thirty-six steps in four turns, and had an overall depth of seven metres and three centimetres. There were signs of fire and the walls and furniture in the rooms were charred.

In Hitler's office the upholstery from the sofa had been cut and remained intact only on the left side. There were bloodstains on the arms of the sofa and on the upholstery there was a stain of blood which penetrated deep through the thickness of the cloth. The stains on the upholstery and the "spray" of blood on the walls were taken away for "further investigation".

Hitler's skull bone discovered in the Soviet archives, the bullet hole clearly visible

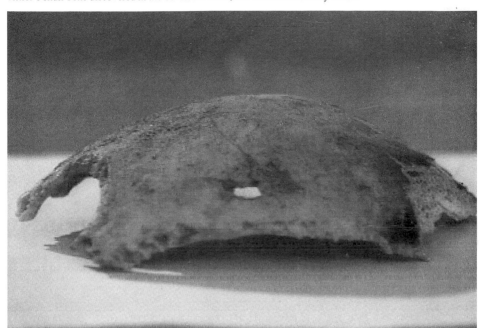

Our independent expert, Professor Viktor Zyagin, examining the skull in the Kremlin in 1995. The six buff-coloured volumes of the Operation Myth File are in the background

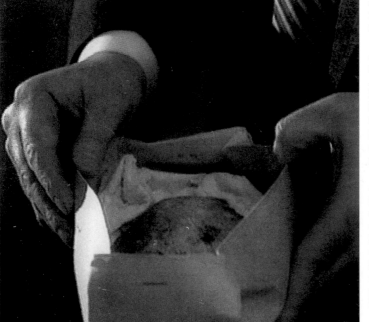

Above: The four skull fragments as they are measured

Left: Sergei Mironenko, a Director of the State Archives of the Russian Federation in Moscow, holding the crumbling box where the skull is kept: the box was originally used for biro refills

Right: Mironenko points out the blood stains on the cross beam of the sofa. The Russians took almost everything they found in the Berlin Bunker – from eyewitnesses to pieces of evidence – back to Moscow in 1945

Inside the Operation Myth File. Mironenko shows photographs of the sofa on which Hitler committed suicide. The accompanying descriptions were added by the Russian investigators

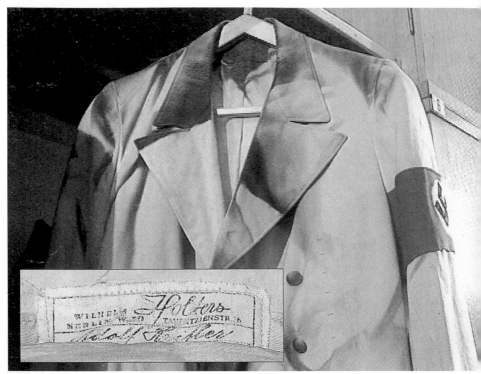

Above: One of Hitler's four fire-scorched uniforms. The red swastika armbands have *Führer, Adolf Hitler* sewn on the reverse side in white silk. *(Inset)* Hitler's name inscibed on the label inside his uniform

The Lubjanka Prison in Moscow: *(above)* the exercise yard of one of the cells where the members of Hitler's entourage were held for interrogation; and *(right)* the view from the guards' walkway looking down over the yards

Semenovsky's conclusion was that the person on the sofa died after his head was struck with a bullet. He came to this conclusion because of the shape of the spray of blood on the wall. It was later established that the blood on the sofa and on the wall was blood of the group A2. Hitler's blood group was A. (In Russia, traditionally the cipher system was used – that is, blood groups were typed 1, 2, 3 or 4. This was then replaced by the letter system, as used in the West – O, A, B, AB. Thus when the forensic experts wrote A2, they were simply confirming that the blood group was A.)

In a document dated 30 May 1946, a report was made on a further excavation of the grave where the corpses of a man and woman had originally been found. No one had expected to find anything important after a year's delay.

"The pit, which had been formed by an aircraft bomb, measured five metres by four metres. It was one metre deep." Then came the second – and much bigger – Russian bombshell 'which we can reveal here for the first time. "At a depth of fifty to sixty cms, two fragments of a skull were found. In one of these fragments there is a bullet hole. The remnants of some cloth and the remnants of a shoe sole, a braided dog collar, and the bones of an unidentified small animal were also found, as were two gasoline canisters." Later on, the report said that the earth in the crater showed some staining, as if it had been hit by shrapnel.

A document dated a day later, 31 May 1946, recorded the investigation of the skull fragments. "Earth is attached to the fragments. The back of the skull and the temple part show signs of fire; they are charred. These fragments belong to an adult. There is an outgoing bullet hole. The shot was fired either in the mouth or the right temple at point blank range. The carbonisation is the result of the fire effect which badly damaged the corpse. Signed Pyotr Semenovsky."

This was obviously a sensational find, the more so as the corpse found in the same crater had lacked part of its skull. Linge had said – as we have revealed for the first time – that only two gasoline canisters had been used to burn the bodies. It looked as though these canisters had been buried alongside the bodies together with Blondi's braided dog collar. The canisters and dog collar didn't prove anything beyond the fact that objects left undiscovered a year before could still be found in 1946. But, in the circumstances, that was important enough.

It began to seem that Semenovsky's commission would clear up the matter of Hitler's death once and for all.

But then things began to go wrong.

In the first place, the documents in the Myth File recorded that the withdrawal of the corpses for a new autopsy was "being delayed". By now these corpses were in the possession of Smersh Counter-Intelligence at its East German headquarters in Magdeburg, safely buried deep below the asphalt-covered courtyard. The documents show that Colonel Klausen, from the Ministry for Internal Affairs, wrote to Abakumov requesting that the two corpses be made available. But they never were and the new autopsies were never carried out: the Commander of Smersh, General Zelenin, refused to release the bodies.

The reason for this refusal is not explained in the documents. Probably it had to do with the rivalry between Smersh and the other security services; or perhaps because Smersh's original autopsies had not settled matters once and for all and they did not want to be proved wrong now. The original autopsies had said that Hitler and Braun had died by poisoning, when it was being put about in the West that Hitler at least had been shot. Since Semenovsky had found a skull with a bullet hole – and everybody in the security services knew it – Smersh stood to be very embarrassed. If, on top of the skull discovery, it was to be proved by a second autopsy that the Hitler or Braun corpses lacked signs of cyanide poisoning, this would represent a failure by Smersh on a grand scale. They had botched this, the most important of all cases.

As a result, Semenovsky gave a measured conclusion to his report. The first examination had not been carried out properly, he said. The base of the skull had not been studied to reveal whether or not Hitler had shot himself in the mouth. Semenovsky also charged the first commission with failing to examine the blood vessels of the throat to see if they had been destroyed by a bullet. Nor had slices been made of the internal organs to test for cyanide compounds. The fact that splinters of a poison ampoule had been found in the corpses' mouths allowed one only to "surmise" that death had been by poisoning. He went on: "Despite all the available evidence, the commission does not think it possible to arrive at a final conclusion. For them, the following things are needed: the exhumation of the corpses; new autopsies; a thorough interrogation of the doctors who knew the peculiarities of Hitler's health and body. That is why we cannot just state: this was Hitler."

Attached to the file were nonetheless a number of personal belongings of Hitler's which had been found either in the Bunker or the Reichschancellery: his golden wristwatch, a medallion given to him by his mother, his Iron Cross for bravery exhibited in World War One and his wound ribbon, awarded after he had been hit in the leg by shrapnel during the same period of military service.

What seems to have happened then is a fudge, Soviet-style. Judging from the wording of Semenovsky's conclusion, he was to avoid taking sides in the dispute between rival security forces yet at the same time still do his job. The phrase "despite all the available evidence", appears to suggest that he was himself convinced that the skull was Hitler's and that therefore the Führer had been shot. At the same time he didn't want to make enemies at Smersh and so stopped just short of saying they had botched the earlier inquiry.

The matter of Hitler's death was kept alive inside Soviet security circles for a little while longer. Linge and Günsche, for example, continued writing their book on *der Chef*. And of course Trevor-Roper's *The Last Days of Hitler* was published the following year, 1947, for general consumption. But within the Soviet hierarchy, the view seems to have taken hold that the matter had been solved: Hitler had been shot, not poisoned, as their own experts had said at first. This was not a politically correct answer – they would have preferred Hitler to have chosen the coward's way out – but there it was. They could not release details of the "correct" second commission without drawing attention to the earlier, "mistaken" first commission. They chose instead to maintain their silence.

The last document in the Hitler archive, the Operation Myth File, is dated 6 August 1948.

One other event needs to be mentioned here, for it completes the picture. It will be recalled that the corpses had been unearthed from the Reichschancellery crater, then re-buried because Klimenko thought that they had already found Hitler's body. The first corpse was, in fact, that of Hitler's doppelgänger. The second corpse was then exhumed when the Intelligence officers realised their mistake. The remains were then taken to Buch for the autopsy where, afterwards, they were buried again, save for the jaws and teeth which were sent to Moscow. Later still, when the Russian unit that had occupied the Buch clinic had withdrawn, the remains – not just of Hitler and Braun but of the Goebbels family, General Krebs and the two dogs as well – had been disinterred a third time and moved to Finow, thirty miles from Berlin, and reburied there.

But this was not the end of the saga. The secret archive continues: "On 3 June 1945, the wooden boxes with the corpses were moved to the vicinity of Ratenow; they were buried at a depth of 1.7 metres. The boxes were positioned in the direction from east to west in the following order: Hitler, Eva Braun, Goebbels, his wife Magda, General Krebs, Goebbels' children. The pit was levelled with the ground and pine trees were planted on the spot. An approximate address: Germany, province of Brandenburg, in the vicinity of Ratenow, a forest to the east of Ratenow, along the highway to Stechow, near the village of Neu Friedrichsdorf, 325 metres from the railway bridge, along the forest lane, to the north-east from a stone landmark with a figure 'iii'.

"On 23 February 1946, this pit was opened and the half-rotten corpses in the wooden boxes were moved to the city of Magdeburg to the place of the deployment of the Third Army of the Soviet Occupation troops. Smersh Counter-Intelligence department buried them in the courtyard at 36, Westerndstrasse, near the southern stone wall of the courtyard, twenty-five metres straight to the east from the wall of the garage, at a depth of two metres. The grave was levelled with the ground. Now the name of the street is Klausenerstrasse."

There the remains achieved a resting place of sorts. They lay in Magdeburg for a quarter of a century. Then in 1970 – by which time only the head of Counter Intelligence at Smersh headquarters in Magdeburg knew what he had beneath him – military necessity intervened again. The Counter Intelligence base was to be returned to East Germany as part of political reconciliation. Now clearly there was at least a potential problem here, if Hitler's grave – albeit a secret one – was being returned to Germany, albeit East Germany which was a Soviet satellite, there was a remote chance that the site would be discovered after all these years. But it was a gamble, a chance that it would become a shrine for neo-fascists. The Russians, a deliberate race, were taking no chances.

The head of the regiment at Magdeburg wrote to Andropov, then head of the KGB, for instruction. Andropov replied promptly on 26 March 1970. His orders were to disinter the corpses, burn them and dispose of the ashes.

Accordingly, Operation Archive was begun. Because the corpses were buried deep and under asphalt, the disinterment was no minor matter. Mechanical digging equipment was required and that would generate noise, a lot of it. A large marquee was therefore erected to keep away prying eyes and a cover story concocted to stop rumours among the locals. It was said that Counter Intelligence had learned that the Nazis had buried some very important documents in the courtyard in 1945. To help the deception, the Hitler excavation was given the codename "Archive".

The disinterment was completed on 4 April 1970. The report on the opening of the grave reads as follows: "Five wooden boxes positioned crosswise had rotted away, turned into 'jellied mass', the remains all mixed with earth.

"Everything was carefully examined. The skulls, vertebrae, bones and ribs were put into new boxes and carried in a truck to the training fields of the Sapper and Armour regiments in the vicinity of Rotten Lake." The bone fragments of Hitler and Braun were all mixed up with those of Krebs, with those of the Goebbels family and the two dogs, so that no one could tell which was which. This, it was felt, was a suitably demeaning end for the high priests of the Third Reich.

The report on the burning of the remains reads as follows: "The destruction was carried out by burning in the fire on the waste ground near Schönebeck, eleven kilometres from Magdeburg. The remains burned away, were ground with the embers into ashes and thrown into one of the Elbe tributaries. The physical destruction of the remains took place in the morning of 5 April." In other words, Counter-Intelligence personnel had worked through the night to ensure that everything was completed at once and no rumours were fuelled.

The tributary of the Elbe at Schönebeck is the Bideriz.

Back in Moscow, we should make it clear that once Ada Petrova had found the skull and the Operation Myth File, her investigations did not stop there. Over the months, acting on this or that tip-off from one archivist or another, she worked her way through no fewer than ten Russian archives (see Appendix B), in the course of which she tracked down far more remains than pieces of the Führer's body, which show how he was killed. For example, she found Hitler's uniforms, she found his photograph album, she found forty-two watercolours by the Führer which show the young Hitler to have been more gifted than many seem willing to concede. Not a great painter – he was twice rejected by the Academy of Fine Arts in Vienna before World War One – but better than is generally thought. She also found incontrovertible proof that relatives of Hitler had been arrested and taken to Soviet Russia where they had died. Whether they were killed or simply died of natural causes is impossible to say. These matters are discussed more fully in the chapters at the end of the book.

Petrova also found some secret Soviet film footage made in May 1945 which showed the state of Reichschancellery garden, the crater where Hitler was buried, the exit from the Bunker, the window where Mengershausen watched the final events and many other incidental details which provide the illustrations for this book. She also obtained rather gruesome film of Goebbels and his wife and children, laid out in a line, the bodies of Josef and Magda badly charred and Josef's left arm jack-knifed in the air.

On the same reel of film there were also shots of Hitler's double. The likeness was unmistakeable, just as was the fact that this man was definitely not Hitler. From the film he appeared to have been shot through the forehead. It was not known whether this was a self-inflicted wound, or whether someone else fired the shot.

The doppelgänger had been identified as one Gustave Weler and it did at least prove once and for all the existence of a double. Apparently, Weler was employed in some fairly menial capacity in the Reichs-chancellery but was infrequently wheeled out to stand in for Hitler much in the same way that General Montgomery is known to have made use of his double.

To summarise the chapter, we can repeat that ten new pieces of information regarding Hitler's death have emerged so far from the documents in the Russian Operation Myth File. They are:

- that Eva Braun escaped to the Reichschancellery garden on the morning of 30 April, for a last look at the sun;
- that Rattenhuber smelled almonds coming from the room;
- that Günsche smelled almonds coming from the death room;
- that Linge saw bloodstains on the walls of the death room;
- that the corpses were still recognisable when Linge went to look at them burning, and that there was a bullet hole in Hitler's skull;
- that Fritz Echtmann said he had produced bridges for *both* Hitler and Eva Braun;
- that Baur constantly changed his story;
- that Günsche saw Hitler grow more worried on 29 April;
- that Günsche himself pulled the body of Eva Braun out of Bunker into the Chancellery garden.

But it is the existence of the skull of Hitler that is the last crucial piece in this saga of detection. Let us now turn to its examination and ask how it refines our understanding of Hitler's last days.

6

BITTER ALMONDS:
THE FORENSIC EVIDENCE

It has to be said that what has gone before, though plain enough, ignores a number of problems in regard to the contradictory evidence concerning the fate of Adolf Hitler and Eva Braun. It is now time to consider this evidence and its associated difficulties. They concern forensic discrepancies, in addition to the various alterations and non-sequiteurs in the verbal testimony of some of the witnesses. Before looking at the skull itself, we should consider in detail the other forensic evidence concerning the corpses retrieved by the Russians from the Bunker.

The initial areas of concern involve discrepancies in Bezymenski's report, who was by no means given access to all available material. The first discrepancy comes from his use of documents which were carefully numbered from 1 to 13. In order to fully appreciate the extent of the problem it may be helpful to set out here in black and white the various autopsy reports as Bezymenski himself did:

Document	1	Autopsy on an "approximately" fifteen year old girl (this was Helga Goebbels who was actually twelve)
	2	Autopsy on Heidi Goebbels (four)
	3	Autopsy on a German shepherd dog (Blondi)
	4	Autopsy on a small black dog
	5	Autopsy on Josef Goebbels
	6	Autopsy on Magda Goebbels
	7	Autopsy on General Krebs
	8	Autopsy on Hedde Goebbels (six)
	9	Autopsy on Holde Goebbels (eight)
	10	Autopsy on Helmut Goebbels (ten)
	11	Autopsy on Hilde Goebbels (eleven)
	12	Autopsy on Adolf Hitler
	13	Autopsy on Eva Braun

This all seems straightforward but, in fact, the documents may be divided into three. The autopsy reports attached to documents 1, 2, 3, 5, 7, 8, 9, 10 and 11 indicated that the smell of bitter almonds was released when organs or tissues were cut into, usually the brain but also the tongue and lungs. As we know, the smell of bitter almonds is a well recognised sign among forensic scientists (and readers of detective novels) of cyanide poisoning. In second place, comes document 13 (Eva Braun): the autopsy report simply records "during autopsy a marked smell of bitter almonds", but does not specify from which organs this smell arose. (It could be, of course, that the Russian scientists were just a little careless in how they wrote up their findings.) And third, the reports for 4 (the small black dog), 6 (Magda Goebbels) and document 12 (Hitler), make no mention of bitter almonds at all. Despite this lack of smell, the autopsies nonetheless did find the presence of cyanide compounds in the dog's internal organs and in Magda Goebbels' internal organs. The autopsy of Hitler made no such mention.

The Russian report makes very little of this difference but others have, suggesting that, despite the presence in the mouth of splinters of glass (which came from a poison ampoule), the lack of a smell of bitter almonds points to the fact that neither Hitler nor Braun was killed by poison: if they had been, the reasoning goes, then the autopsies would not have failed to mention that poison was present in the internal organs. This discrepancy will be addressed in more detail later on, but it is worth noting here that both the reports on the black dog and on Magda Goebbels failed to mention the smell of bitter almonds during dissection and yet still found cyanide compounds in the internal organs. Given that there was a smell of bitter almonds during Eva Braun's autopsy, albeit from an unspecified area, the possibility must also exist that the Russian investigators were simply sloppy and inconsistent in their *wording* rather than their procedure.

Bezymenski's second problem area specifically concerns the corpse of Eva Braun. As the Russian themselves noted, the upper lobe of the left lung in this corpse showed two large perforations. Also, in the left pleural cavity there were six steel fragments measuring up to (half a square cm – shrapnel. Moreover, in the upper frontal part of the pericardium were two apertures surrounded by "a clearly discernible haemorrhage". In other words, this corpse had been hit by shrapnel, the haemorrhage indicating that the blow had been suffered while there was sufficient blood pressure to form a haemorrhage – that is to say, when the body *was alive.*

A third doubt concerns two matters highlighted by the second commission. It reported blood not only in Hitler's living room, where he was supposed to have committed suicide, but also on his bed in the next room. Was this blood shed at the same time as the blood in the living room and if so how did it get there?

Each of these discrepancies – plus the fact that the Russians themselves had so many reservations about their findings – when added to the large number of changes in the testimony of Linge, Günsche and the others from the Bunker introduces more and more doubt into the whole issue.

On top of this, another layer of theory – the fourth – about what really happened in those last days of Hitler has very recently been aired. This time the theoriser is Hugh Thomas, an English surgeon of international repute who is an authority on gunshot wounds. In 1979, Dr Thomas created a furore with a book which claimed that the prisoner of war in Spandau Prison, Berlin, was *not* Rudolf Hess. Dr Thomas has taken a great interest in Hitler's demise and explored thoroughly the forensic evidence. His book, *Doppelgänger: The Truth About the Bodies in the Berlin Bunker* was published in 1995. Thomas was given access to some parts of the Operation Myth File, discussed in the last chapter. But he has not had access to Hitler's skull or any of the other remains, as we have. It is a pity that we, as non-specialists, were given access when Dr Thomas, the trained forensic specialist, was not. We are all interested in ascertaining the historical truth.

His view is that the deaths of Adolf Hitler and Eva Braun were the subject of a complicated forensic fraud in which the corpses burned outside the bunker were *not* the corpses of the Führer and his wife. Dr Thomas starts with the set of circumstances mentioned above – that Braun, according to the Soviet documents and autopsy, must have been killed by shrapnel which spattered the chest rather than by cyanide poisoning. He says that the kind of haemorrhage which occurred in the lungs could only have been sustained when there was still enough pressure in the blood vessels to force blood out.

Thomas then goes on to examine the dental evidence which was recorded in the Soviet autopsy on the Eva Braun corpse. Document 13 in Bezymenski's report said that in the upper jaw two teeth were found on the right side (a molar and the prong of a tooth with a broad socket), and three on the left (a loose canine and two molars). The others were missing.

On the lower jaw, no teeth were found on the right side – probably because of burning – and on the left side the second incisor, the canine tooth, two bicuspids and two molars were all preserved, all of them moderately worn, and showing "visible changes due to dental caries". Under the tongue a gold bridge was found, unattached, which connected the second right bicuspid and the third right molar by means of a gold crown.

Thomas found even what he read about about the tooth remains was unusual. It was odd, he says, that so many teeth were missing, because tooth enamel is very fire resistant. It is very rare for a fire to destroy so many teeth. The fact that teeth were lying between the tongue and the palate was also curious – if the upper teeth were to come loose they would presumably fall down the oral cavity, either into the throat or the lower jaw, depending on the position of the corpse. Such evidence could not be conclusive of course and nor does Dr Thomas, in his detached analysis, claim that it is. Next he turns to the dental diagram of Braun's teeth which had been drawn up by Professor Hugo Blaschke. These records had been captured by the Western Allies and proves, according to Dr Thomas, that the teeth found on the body of Eva Braun could not be hers. Blaschke had told the Allies that he had last treated Braun in March 1945 when her teeth were in good shape, with few fillings and no false teeth. In particular, there was little caries in evidence, unlike the teeth on the corpse; the upper right molar, which was intact on the corpse, should have had a filling had it been Eva Braun's.

Then there was the question of the gold bridge. This was found, according to the Soviet documents, "under the tongue, unattached". It was designed to connect the second right bicuspid and the third right molar by means of a gold crown. The first and second artificial molars were attached on the front. This bridge was designed to fit part of the jaw that was missing but Thomas argued that Blaschke's drawings of Braun's teeth did not indicate any such bridge construction, nor any appropriate dental preparation in the adjoining teeth to accommodate "any form of bridge".

Before we consider this development, we need to cast our minds back again to 1945. On 9 May Soviet troops had located Käthe Heusermann and Fritz Echtmann, respectively the dental nurse who had assisted Dr Blaschke and the technician who had actually made the dental prostheses for both Hitler and Braun. Both testified that *two* bridges had been made for Braun and Hitler, identical in each case, the second in each case as a reserve in case anything should go wrong with the first one. Soviet records also said that a box of gold crowns and duplicate bridges (in the plural), for Hitler and Braun, had been found in the Chancellery dental office. Later, Käthe Heusermann said that the box in the Chancellery had only contained one bridge for Eva but that the other one, to her knowledge, had never been fitted.

On the face of it, Dr Thomas's suspicions seem borne out – that one bridge was put into the mouth of a "decoy" corpse to make the Russian authorities believe the body was Eva's.

Dr Thomas says that Blaschke's dental diagram of Braun showed absolutely no evidence of dental caries, cavities or other dental defects, or any bridge construction. And yet, Heusermann's interrogation – seen by us in the course of writing this book – says she attended Braun on several occasions, that the sixth and seventh teeth in Braun's lower jaw were missing and, most crucially, that Heusermann had been present when Professor Blaschke *fitted* one of the gold bridges. "The bridge rested on the golden cemented crown put on the eighth tooth on the right side and on the golden fastening on the fifth tooth on the right side . . . I clearly remember the golden bridge . . . because I was holding this bridge in my hands and rinsing it with alcohol before it was fixed." Surely this casts doubt on Professor Blaschke's memory of the state of Braun's teeth and puts pay to the theory that the bridge in the female corpse had been left there as part of some forensic fakery.

But Dr Thomas feels sure the shrapnel wounds in the chest and the poor match of the teeth, together with the gold bridge, proves that the body of the so-called Eva Braun is in fact an example of forensic fraud. He believes that this fraud was perfected over a long period of time and that Braun had escaped from the Bunker at the very end, presumably living on in anonymity or being killed at a later date. In putting forward this hypothesis, Thomas is forced to concede that this plan would have involved the long-term deception of Hitler. For all witnesses were agreed that Eva Braun appeared for the final farewell ceremony, after the lunch at which she was *not* present. For this theory to stand up, *everyone* in the Bunker would have to have been part of the conspiracy – except for Hitler. Is this really likely?

Hugh Thomas now turns his attention to the corpse of the Führer. In this case his suspicions were first aroused by the fact that the remains, as Bezymenski said, were lacking a left foot. For bones like that to have been consumed by fire, he says, a temperature of more than 1000 degrees centigrade would have been needed, far beyond what could have occurred in the open garden of the Reichschancellery. He then refers to a document by one of the original Soviet investigators – not seen by the authors of this book – to the effect that he had initial suspicions that the loss might have been due to a congenital defect or an accident.

Again, however, Dr Thomas concentrates on the teeth. A bridge connecting nine teeth of the upper jaw was found on the corpse. It was anchored by pins on the second left and second right incisors. The bridge had been sawed across behind the first left bicupsid. Thomas believes that his upper jaw bridge was lying loose in the oral cavity. He also says that the Soviet archives revealed that the colour of the teeth was "surprisingly good" for teeth that had withstood a petrol fire.

The dental assistant Heusermann told the Russian authorities in 1945 that the upper bridge that Hitler had had fitted had been sawn through *in situ* in October 1944 when he had a problem with an abcess. Thomas therefore concludes that much the same had happened with Hitler as he concluded had happened with Braun, namely that again a duplicate bridge had been placed in the corpse of someone else. The fact that the saw mark had been duplicated, only showed that the whole fraud had been perpetrated by a professional dentist and some-one who had access to the Führer's dental records. This would seem to narrow the field greatly, perhaps to Blaschke and/or Kunz, the man who had been accused of helping murder the six Goebbels children.

Regarding the lower jaw, the fraud procedure was more complicated still. For here a jaw was found with five real teeth attached, in the same places as Hitler had real teeth, and gold bridgework covering four teeth on the left side and six on the right. There was also evidence, suggests Thomas, that the jaw showed evidence of recent tooth extraction, when Hitler had had none.

There are holes in this theory, of course. One is that it would have taken some time to manufacture such a jaw, but yet Hitler did not decide to stay in Berlin and commit suicide in the way that he did until 22 April. A further drawback is that the Russians undoubtedly did find some gold bridges in the Reichschancellery dental office which belonged to Hitler and Braun. Given that the (live) Hitler was pre-sumably still wearing the ones that had been fitted, then the duplicates must have been used in the "Hitler" corpse and one of the Braun bridges in the "Braun" corpse. That would only have left one bridge – Eva Braun's – in the box in the Reichschancellery to be found by the Soviets. And yet the evidence that we are now able to present in this book for the first time shows that Fritz Echtmann identified in the Reichschancellery dental office duplicate bridges for Hitler *and* Braun. This part of Thomas's theory, at least, does not stand up.

There is also the fact that the jaws in the Hitler corpse were not found loose, in the sense that the gold bridge was loose in Eva Braun's jaw. It will be remembered that the autopsy said that the tongue was held firmly by the upper and lower jaw, so that if anything was loose it was this entire structure. This would presumably be a very difficult arrangement to fake, for how would it be held together prior to being inserted into the oral cavity?

In fact, Thomas seems to go back on his own reasoning at this point, certainly so far as Hitler is concerned. For in the end, Dr Thomas does conclude that the male body in the crater was in all probability Hitler's – owing to the simple fact that, in his physical and psycho logical state, the Führer could never have escaped. We have already raised the issue that the Soviet autopsy reports can be read too literally, overlooking the fact that perhaps those records were themselves somewhat lackadaisical in their reporting of detail so that what appear to be important omissions are nothing of the kind. Hugh Thomas choses to see the failure to report the smell of bitter almonds when dissecting Braun and Hitler as something that should have alerted the Soviet authorities to the fact that the corpses of the "alleged Eva" and the "alleged Adolf" did not die of cyanide poisoning. Ampoules had been placed in their mouths and crushed, *but after death*. The fraudulent purpose here was to create the picture that they had died in this way and divert attention from what had really taken place. Dr Thomas makes much of the different shapes of the splinters found in the mouths of the Goebbels children on the one hand, and Blondi, "Hitler" and "Eva" on the other. In the case of the children the glass fragments had been ground by the gnashing of their teeth, in their death spasms, whereas "Hitler's" and "Eva's" were less ground down, as if they had been crushed by someone using pliers or forceps just as when Dr Haase had helped to kill Blondi.

The only trouble with this explanation is that it is partial. We should not forget that the six children had been drugged first, to avoid knowledge and pain of death. How, therefore, could they have ground down the ampoules in their death throes when specific measures had been taken to avoid that? Misch actually said in his testimony that Magda Goebbels had ground down the capsules herself and placed them in her children's mouths. Furthermore, the autopsy on the small black dog showed that it had traces of cyanide compounds in its internal organs but "no foreign objects" (no splinters of ampoule) in its muzzle. Third, splinters of glass had been found in the mouth of Frau Goebbels but no mention was made in her autopsy of the smell of bitter almonds. These descriptions *prove* nothing, but they do show that the Soviet autopsy report writers varied in the way they put their reports together. Too much should not be made of a literal reading of reports written fifty years ago.

In trying to work out what had really happened in the Bunker, Hugh Thomas next turns his attention to the remains of blood in Hitler's suite, which he believes corroborate his theory of forensic fraud. Here his reasoning is fairly straightforward. If Hitler and Braun poisoned themselves there should be no blood in the room. If, however, Hitler shot himself through the head, there should be at least some blood on the sofa where he was found, on the walls around him and perhaps on the floor. The first Russian commission does not appear to have examined this question but the second commission did. At one stage, that report reads as follows: "Blood on the wall and on the sofa resulted from a head wound caused by gunshot on the subject who was sitting on the right of the sofa." We also now have Linge's testimony – reported in this book in detail for the first time – that there *was* blood on the floor, on the walls and on the sofa, where it was so thick that it had soaked right through the cloth covering.

But Thomas is unwilling to accept this evidence at face value. He thinks that the second commission report was fabricated.In his opinion, Semenovsky would have been unlikely to comment in this way because, at the time this paragraph was written, he had not received the blood analysis. Moreover, as a professional, Semenovsky would have been cautious in confirming that the stains, now nearly a year old, were in fact blood. Logically, this makes sense, although there is perhaps little point in second-guessing Semenovsky at this distance. He was clearly under pressure to report and what else could the stains have been in that position? The records we have seen show that the stains were tested not once but twice – by a Dr Rosanova – and in both cases found to be composed of human blood, type A.

Dr Thomas is not convinced, even by the blood analysis, especially as this blood group, he says, does not match those of the corpses. This is interesting, because he doesn't say what the blood groups of the corpses were and of course Semenovsky never had chance to examine the corpses. Thomas never had the opportunity to examine them either, yet nevertheless gives the blood group of the blood on the bed and sofa – A – but not of the corpses.

Still on the question of the blood, he doesn't address the evidence of Lieutenant-Colonel W. Byford-Jones, who had observed quite a lot of blood on the walls, floor and sofa of Hitler's living room in August 1945.

Now let us move forward to a related issue and one which Thomas, quite rightly perhaps, regards as more important. This is the fact that there was blood, not only on the sofa in Hitler's living room, but also on the bed in his bedroom. Why should this have been, given Linge's and Günsche's testimony and those of the others? None of the eyewitnesses had mentioned going anywhere near Hitler's bedroom.

Thomas also says that there was in fact not much blood in Hitler's living room, just a few stains on the right arm of the sofa (the right as you sat in it) and on the crossbar. He also noted that the blood stains on the bed were about half way along, and gave the appearance of trickling down. He therefore comes to the conclusion that these were consistent with a suicide attempt by Eva Braun. On this scenario, Thomas has Eva slitting her wrists and lying on the bed in Hitler's bedroom in a *fake* suicide attempt, so as to "officially incapacitate" herself and make her unable to go through with any suicide pact.

As supporting evidence, Thomas points to Linge's initial testimony in which he had claimed that they provided only one blanket for the corpses "and was very vague about carrying a second corpse". This, Thomas suggests, points to the fact that Eva was to be spared.

But does it really? In the first place, Linge's testimony in Russia – and as we have reported here for the first time – showed that there *was* a lot of blood in the living room. Second, if the other corpse was *not* Eva Braun then surely there would have been an even more pressing need for two blankets so as to hide the features of the female cadaver? Where would the "replacement corpse" have come from? Presumably, in those final, terrible days, corpses inside the Reichschancellery or the immediate vicinity were not unknown. But this one would have to have been brought into the Bunker, clothed in Eva's blue dress and then taken out again. The real Eva, meanwhile, having a few moments before slitting her wrists in a fake suicide attempt, would have been spirited away out of the Bunker at a time when no one else was leaving, rather than waiting instead for the mass break-out that came more than a day later. Surely this is an unlikely scenario.

But how did blood get on to the bed? We cannot say for certain but in his testimony reported earlier, Linge said that the furniture in the living room at least was moved to make room for the laying out of Hitler's and Braun's corpses, so that they could be covered in blankets. The bedroom was next door. Conditions were cramped. People were on edge. Maybe the corpse with blood on it was laid on or near the bed. Alternatively, consider the fact that Hitler shot himself in the head: blood might shoot anywhere. The Bunker rooms were very small and the bedroom was next door, just through a doorway. Thirdly, the blood on the bed may have arrived there in other ways on a quite separate occasion, nothing to do with the last day.

Thomas's final argument in this new theory concerns the actual mode of death for Hitler. "Hitler was not poisoned," he says. "He was not shot, so how *did* he die? We are left to consider only one real practical alternative; the forceful *strangling* of the Führer." According to Dr Thomas: "We can envisage Hitler shuffling across to speak to Goebbels – eyes water-filled and yet demonic, his face flushed and covered with rivulets of dried tears, with spittle running down from the corner of his mouth." People around Hitler know what is coming and, on Rattenhuber's orders, the Bunker is cleared. They have been given their rations and are instructed not to come back until told to do so. Linge discovers Eva Braun, sitting on the sofa in Hitler's living room, having slit her wrists, dripping blood on to the arm of the sofa. He lifts her from the sofa, takes her next door, into Hitler's bedroom, leaves her there, where she continues to bleed on to the bed and its wooden supports.

Linge fetches Stumpfegger, who staunches her blood loss with tape. Hitler is aware that something is going on and demands to be told. At this point, Linge tells the Führer about the suicide attempt and offers him a poison capsule. "Glancing blankly and uncomprehendingly at his manservant, Hitler calls him a 'stupid peasant' and turns his back."

At this, according to Hugh Thomas, Linge grasps the cyanide capsule himself and then grabs Hitler, trying to force the capsule into his mouth from behind. A struggle ensues. Linge fails to get the capsule into Hitler's mouth and so, knowing that the end is near for all of them, he closes his hands around the Führer's throat. Hitler, though aged only fifty-six, has aged prematurely and cannot resist. Linge strangles him.

Linge then calls for Stumpfegger who checks that Hitler is dead, then places a cyanide ampule in his mouth and crushes it with a pair of forceps. The dummy Eva is now brought down in to the Bunker where, in Eva's own bedroom, it is dressed in her blue dress which has been got ready for the purpose, its black slit open. The fake Eva is then put with the real Hitler on the sofa in his living room, while the real Eva is told that her husband has committed suicide. "She doesn't even seem aware of events as she is smuggled up the back stairs," Thomas speculates.

Linge now goes out of the suite, leaving the two corpses wrapped in blankets, and informs the others in the Bunker of the "double suicide". Some of those others have their suspicions about what went on but they also have their own reasons for not prying too much. Several notice that as Linge keeps repeating "the Führer is dead", he makes no mention of Eva Braun.

"The funeral and the funeral pyre go to plan, and the SS dentist Kunz briefly attends to place a gold bridge under the tongue of the fake Eva, completing the forensic deception, before she is heaved off a canvas sling into the shell crater to be lightly covered with earth, rubble and rubbish."

The thing about this theory is that even Dr Thomas himself admits there is absolutely *no* evidence to support it. *Doppelgänger* is entirely devoted to a detailed and in many respects impressive analysis of the forensic evidence surrounding the deaths of thirteen individuals in the Bunker. Yet at the end, all Thomas can offer is speculation.

Introducing his strangling theory, he again admits: "We are now free to indulge in what it must be admitted is relatively uninformed speculation – an alternative scenario for the death of Hitler, inside the Bunker.

"I defend this exercise on the grounds that, as it is at least based on a background of forensic data, as an alternative it cannot be less truthful or less accurate than the story that has been accepted to date. However, it has a fatal flaw in that it is based on supposed logic, and it is all too easy to delude oneself that one is being logical and lay oneself open to ridicule. I am nevertheless convinced that even a ridiculed alternative is better than a discredited historical fiction."

So that is the latest theory – the fourth – about Hitler's end, published in April 1995. Thomas' conclusion is that the Führer was strangled and Eva got away. (Where Eva went to, incidentally, Thomas does not say. He seems content to accept the fact that, since other prominent Nazis – Koch, Gehlen, Eichmann, Mengele, not to mention Bormann – remained outside allied custody for a number of years, Eva could have done the same. Perhaps.)

There is a sense of an open season on Hitler, perhaps, with new theories produced every few years. All this may be fun, but does it really advance our historical knowledge? In fact, Hugh Thomas has done us a service in publishing his new theory, unlikely as we consider it is. In drawing attention to the medical and forensic evidence in the way that he has, we are now able to consider certain aspects of the chain of events in a new light. We believe his theories have helped us to approximate the truth. For what Thomas' evidence signally fails to address is the *psychology* of the last days in the Bunker. And therein, we suggest, lies the crucial clue.

7

1995: PROFESSOR ZYAGIN'S INDEPENDENT VERDICT

In writing this book, two facts seem of crucial importance to us in understanding what went on in the Berlin Bunker. And they are *facts*, as opposed to conjecture, as we intend to show.

The first is that the Bunker was a small place. A very small, claustrophobic place. James O'Donnell, who visited the Bunker in 1945 and later devoted an entire book to the structure, described it as: "ghostly and bleak. All the ceilings were low and the corridors were like the narrow passages in a crypt. A few of the thirty-odd cramped rooms had been painted battleship grey; the rough corridor walls were a rusty brown. In places, the bare cement dripped moisture; the masons had never been able to finish their plastering work. Three rooms, only slightly larger than the rest, ten by fifteen feet, plus a toilet and shower, were Hitler's private quarters."

Hitler had barely left the Bunker and Reichschancellery grounds since mid-January 1945. By April, conditions were worse than primitive. Electric cables ran across the floors in a tangled mess, the sewers failed regularly, all the women shared Eva Braun's lavatory, there was a smell of dogs and human body odour, there were stale sandwiches and beer cans left to litter the corridors, and a pungent smell of coal-tar disinfectant. Someone told James O'Donnell it was like "working in a public urinal".

When one considers the layout of the upper and lower Bunkers – which both had central corridors nearly always occupied by several people – and when that is added to the fact that the dimensions were so small, it becomes very clear that life below the Reichschancellery garden was very intimate indeed. There was scope for private conversations, of course, but everyone always knew that these private conversations were taking place. Two sentries stood guard at the spiral staircase, so that all movement between the two bunkers was observed. All the private rooms led off the central corridors and, except for

Goebbels' and Dr Stumpfegger's rooms, did not lead from one set of quarters to another without going via the corridor.

In other words, privacy was impossible. Everyone knew everyone else's business, it was impossible to hide. This is clearly of great importance to the events of the last days. If any plans called for secrecy, with only some of the inhabitants being admitted to the confidence, this would have been difficult, if not impossible to maintain. Others may not have known the details, but they would have known that something was afoot.

It is easy to overlook how the cramped conditions of the Bunker would have influenced events. After O'Donnell and Byford-Jones were lucky enough to visit it, the structure was designated off-limits for all but those with special authorisation for many years. It was blown up by the Russians after the second commission completed its work.

The second crucial fact in trying to understand what happened, is the murder of the Goebbels children. At the risk of overstressing the point, this was probably the single most horrific act in the Bunker – if the murder of six children can be called a single act.

Whoever performed the murders – whether it was Kunz, Stumpfegger or Magda Goebbels herself – it is clear that the children's mother took a significant part in what happened. There is no suggestion that she was the victim of a trick and therefore was not aware that her children were to die. There is no suggestion from anyone that the children were killed against her will.

This is not to say that she was happy with the killings. Trevor-Roper says that she was not present at the final farewell ceremony, when Hitler and Eva Braun took their leave of her husband, Bormann, Burgdorf, Krebs and the various secretaries in the central corridor. "Unnerved by the approaching death of her children, she remained all day in her own room," he wrote.

O'Donnell tells us more. He says that two plans had been mooted to save Magda Goebbels "and her brood". One had been conceived by Speer and stemmed from the fact that the Goebbels' family home was at Schwanenwerder, a peninsula in the meandering Havel river which flows into the Elbe. Speer wanted to whisk Magda and the children aboard a barge and to float it down the Havel to the Elbe, where the Americans had arrived on 11 April. Speer had kept this plan from Goebbels himself because he feared the Propaganda Minister would veto it. However, another plan, which also involved escape by barge and was devised by Werner Naumann, was put to Goebbels, who approved. Naumann's barge was to serve as a hiding place for Magda and the children, in the reeds of the Havel, until the worst was over. O'Donnell goes on. "It was the distraught but adamant mother who rejected both plans out of hand, saying that she must refuse to abandon her husband. She also stated that she was determined to die with the Führer and take her children with her 'because my darlings are simply too good for this bad world'." (Mohnke too had offered to put a tank at their disposal. Maria Kimmich, Goebbels' younger sister who was in Berlin, would have taken the children, as would have Liesl Ostertag.)

O'Donnell's researches also uncovered the fact that there were in fact two cliques in the Bunker in the last days. There was an Alpine Redoubt clique, led by Bormann, who "yearned" to decamp to Berchtesgaden. They had caught the Führer in a weak moment on 29 March, "when he seemed to be suddenly overcome by a desire for the air of the OberSalzberg." Hearing of this, Goebbels, who epitomised the second clique, hurried over to the Bunker where, according to Günsche: "Goebbels, clutching his Führer by both lapels, implored him to remember the solemn oath that he had once sworn, with Goebbels, towards midnight on 30 January 1933, the day Hitler had become Chancellor and entered the Old Reich Chancellery: 'We shall never abandon this building voluntarily. No power in this world can ever drive us out!'" Goebbels never, for a moment, doubted the Hitler myth that he had helped to create. And, as part of that myth, Hitler had to die, and die at the last, in Berlin, in the Reichschancellery, in the Bunker.

After Goebbels and his family moved into the Bunker at Hitler's request on 22 April, he found that he had more time on his hands. Writes O'Donnell: "Bunker inmates reported that he spent long hours reading and writing, in his office next to Hitler's . . . he attended the military briefings. Goebbels now found, too, that he had abundant time for his children, played games and sang songs. This was not just an act – Goebbels was genuinely fond of his children – but it added to the stupefying unreality, as Liesl Ostertag, Eva Braun's maid from Berchtesgaden reported: 'You simply could not watch those touching family scenes and still believe this doting father had multiple murder in his heart'."

On 29 April, the day before Hitler died, Goebbels gave a small party in the cellar of the New Reichschancellery. "It was, he said, to be his last farewell, and that of his family, to the Berliners among whom they had lived through all the War years." There were about forty guests, some nurses, young boys and girls, some wounded soldiers. One boy from the Hitler Youth, in uniform, sang a song while accompanying himself on the accordion:

Die blauen Dragoner, sie reiten
mit klingendem Spiel durch das Tor.
Fanfaren sie begleiten
hell zu den Huegeln empor . . .

The blue dragoons, they are riding
Through the gate as music thrills.
Fanfares are their companions
As proudly they ride to the hills . . .

The entire Goebbels family was present at the party, seated together at a long oak table: "All joined in and lustily repeated the chorus."

O'Donnell was convinced that Magda Goebbels had killed her own children. After she had done the deed, Rochus Misch claimed that her blue eyes were tinged with red. She smoked, but did not speak. She took some champagne and began playing solitaire. Artur Axmann confirmed that when he had seen the Goebbels at the long conference table, at around 6.30 pm on 1 May, she was chain-smoking and sipping champagne. She held her head high but said little. Axmann was told by others that the children were already dead.

Then there is the question of Magda turning up in Hitler's part of the Bunker just as he was about to kill himself, when she burst past Günsche and pleaded with the Führer to leave the Bunker and fly south to Berchtesgaden.

This – and her last-minute attempt to prevent Hitler committing suicide – paints a consistent picture of Magda Goebbels. She was an ardent Nazi, yes, and maybe had the touch of fanaticism about her. But she was also a mother, who approached the death of her six children with fierce pride at one moment and severe doubts the next. She could find the strength to look upon her deed with ardour at one moment and recoil the next, weeping, drinking, chain-smoking and seeking solace in cards. She could speak about her children being born for the Third Reich on any number of occasions but even at the final moment she begged the Führer to fly to Berchtesgaden: if the Führer fled, then her children would not have to die.

Finally, let us consider the death of Magda and Josef Goebbels, as pieced together by James O'Donnell. He says that they had both carefully rehearsed Professor Haase's approved Bunker method, pistol and poison. "Magda went first. She bit into her capsule, sank slowly to the soft spring earth. Her husband fired a bullet into the back of her blonde head. Goebbels then bit into his own capsule, squeezed the trigger of his Walther P-38 pistol, and put a bullet through his right temple."

To us, as authors, a simple psychological truth stands out a mile against these reports. It is not proof like forensic evidence can be proof but the truth it encapsulates is much more profound, far more powerful. Given the small, cramped conditions of the Bunker, making secrecy impossible, and Magda Goebbels' vacillating nature – added to the fact that her own death did not follow immediately on Hitler's but at a distance of twenty-four hours – is it *at all likely* that she would have allowed her children to die if there had been the slightest doubt about Hitler's own death? The answer is glaringly obvious: she would not. In her moments of weakness, she was looking for a way out as late as the afternoon of 30 April when she burst into Hitler's quarters. She carried out the killing of her "brood" with evident emotion. O'Donnell's verdict, that she killed the children herself, is almost certainly correct. If the Führer had died, murdering her own children now became almost a matter of duty. But because she loved her children, killing them herself was a last, loving act. To have left it to others would have been callous, an abrogation of responsibility which would have been out of character.

According to Trevor-Roper, Artur Axmann, who had been too late for the farewell ceremony, was nonetheless admitted to Hitler's private suite to see the dead bodies: "He examined them, and stayed in the room for some minutes, talking with Goebbels." According to O'Donnell – quoting Günsche and Axmann interviewed in the 1970s – Bormann led the way into Hitler's suite, followed by the small group of Linge, Günsche, Goebbels and Axmann. Linge's testimony also placed Goebbels as part of the group that waited outside Hitler's suite while the suicides took place, and confirmed that he was part of the group that entered the living room after a short delay.

To us, there seems little doubt that Goebbels was in a position to verify the Führer's death. Had there been the slightest doubt about it, would he have allowed his wife to go ahead?

What about Eva Braun? Here again the same arguments apply.

Goebbels was there, in Hitler's living room. He saw the bodies. This is the strongest evidence that Eva Braun died, but there is more. It is known that Goebbels never really liked Braun. She had often overruled his judgement about what films Hitler should be shown in the Reichschancellery and, on a number of occasions, he had considered her over-eager to act as nanny to his children. A propaganda wizard, Goebbels had spent the War making sure Eva stayed out of the limelight, in order to keep alive the Führer's solitary charisma, based on the fact that "he was desired by all but possessed by none." And yet here was Eva, in the last days, finally getting her own way and marrying Adolf. As for Magda, she was not a little envious of Eva. In love with the Führer herself, Frau Goebbels hated the fact that, at the end, Eva bore his name. In these circumstances, one asks oneself again if it is conceivable that Goebbels, or his wife, would have countenanced killing their children, or themselves, if there had been any doubt about Eva Braun's death. Of course not. The myth, which was Goebbels' creation as much as anybody's, would have been punctured.

Then there is the psychology and behaviour of Eva Braun herself. Remember that she had returned to Berlin on 15 April against Hitler's orders and refused to leave. She loved him and was now demonstrating her love and loyalty. Hitler had said in his last days – according to Hugh Trevor-Roper – that only Eva Braun and his dog Blondi had remained faithful to him.

There was also Braun's behaviour inside the Reichschancellery after she had arrived. Together with some of the young secretaries, she took pistol practice on an emergency range set up in the yard of Goebbels' Propaganda Ministry, across Wilhelmstrasse and next to the Chancellery. More relevant perhaps were Speer's observations when he visited the Bunker for the last time on 23 April. He had been friendly with Eva for some years, their friendship based on a love of skiing and the outdoors, and he had designed a dresser for her some years before, which was now in the Bunker, looking a little out of place in the cramped conditions. When they met, it was close to midnight and Speer had been in the Bunker since 4 the preceding morning without anyone offering him anything to eat or drink. Eva did not forget her manners, however, and arranged a snack of biscuits and champagne.

Speer observed that Eva was the only Bunker inmate: "who seemed even remotely happy. Her quiet calm was not merely play-acting. It was a serenity, Speer felt, not unmixed with exultation on the part of a woman who, if only in a morbid pact, like that of Tristan and Isolde, was finally going to meet her death with the man she loved." Eva told Speer with obvious pride about how Hitler had tried to persuade her to leave the Bunker and how her categorical refusal had pleased him.

Once again, it may be necessary to point out that these psychological factors are not *proof* of anything, in the sense that teeth remains or blood groupings or the smell of bitter almonds may be proof of something. But in those last days in the Berlin Bunker, as elsewhere at other times, people acted as they did *for a reason*. And in order to judge the rest of the evidence we need a commonsensical understanding of the motives of people around Hitler, as well as of Hitler himself.

Much has been made of the fact that several of the most important witnesses to the last days of Hitler, people who were in the Bunker, have changed their testimony. We have already highlighted discrepancies in various testimonies. We do not need to repeat our explanation for such contradictions again here. But we do need to examine the potentially sinister possibility that there was a widespread conspiracy among the survivors of the Bunker to concoct a completely spurious version of events in order to mislead the Allies.

We think we can immediately dismiss the idea that it was concocted because Hitler and/or Braun escaped. The psychological analysis of Braun and the Goebbels family dismiss that theory. No, if this conspiracy existed, it would have needed to call within its ambit not only Linge, Günsche, Baur, Bormann, Goebbels, Voss, Axmann and many others such as the secretaries who worked inside the Bunker, but also those regular soldiers outside in the Reichschancellery proper – Mansfeld, Karnau, Mengershausen, Hilco Poppen. This might perhaps be possible – just – given a certain amount of time to brief everyone, and assuming that someone, who was in overall control, knew in advance what was going to happen. But was that the case? Highly unlikely. No one knew for certain that Hitler was going to kill himself before it happened. His plan to do so was by then a week old only, but no one knew exactly when he was going to kill himself or how.

To be sure, the occupants of the Bunker had more than a day to get their story coordinated after the event before the break-out began. But from their point of view the situation would not have been helped by the fact that some of the occupants were captured by the Western Allies and some by the Russians. One half didn't know what the other half was saying, they didn't know who was being tortured, what forensic evidence had been found. They did not even know who else had been captured and who had not. And never forget that the War wasn't over. The situation for POWs was very uncertain.

In these extremely uncertain circumstances, we think there can be little doubt that any last-minute concocted plan would have come apart – and sooner rather than later. When asked the details of the plan, different people would have given different and contradictory replies. The sham would have been quickly exposed, for not more than a day's preparation could have gone into the briefings of the various people.

If Mengershausen, Karnau, Poppen and Mansfeld were part of the plot, it was impressively organised. But the natural thing surely would have been to limit the number of people who took part. The more there were, the greater the chances of a security leak.

In considering a conspiracy theory, we need to return to the fact that the most important witnesses – Kempka, Linge, Günsche and Baur – each changed their stories. We may start with Hitler's driver, Kempka, where the evidence is clearest. His evidence was the basis for Trevor-Roper's *The Last Days of Hitler*, the conclusion of which was that Hitler shot himself through the mouth and Eva Braun poisoned herself. In 1973, however, Kempka confessed to James O'Donnell that: "in 1945, to save my own skin, I told American and British interrogators just about anything or everything I thought they wanted to hear. Since they kept grilling me about 'that shot' I finally told them that I had heard it. It seemed to make things easier."

It is possible, of course, that Kempka was lying on the *second* occasion – or on both – and we shall return to this possibility. But, for the moment, let us accept Kempka's reasons for changing his story. Now let us turn to Hitler's personal pilot, Baur. He was described by O'Donnell as "bumptious" and, by Albert Speer, as "pig-headed and stupid . . . unteachable, a keeper of the flame". When he was released from Soviet captivity on 8 October 1955, he had this to say about Hitler's death: "The Führer looked me gravely in the eyes, shook my hand, said goodbye and shot himself. Eva Braun shot herself at the same time. I did not stay to see the bodies afterwards and do not know what happened to them."

Was this testimony to be believed? The short answer is "no", for his claim to have been present in the Bunker contradicts the testimony of several others, who say he was elsewhere in the Reichschancellery, recovering from the canteen party the night – or rather early morning – before. Additionally, the testimony of Baur, taken in Russia – and presented here in this book for the first time – shows how often he contradicted himself and why. (He was afraid.) The same reservations therefore apply to his claims that, shortly before midnight on 30 April, Rattenhuber sent a soldier to the Chancellery garden to examine the state of Hitler's and Braun's corpses. According to Baur, the man reported back that: "both bodies have now been so burned that only very small remnants still remain. These are unrecognisable." As Hugh Thomas and others have pointed out, the temperatures in the crater in the Chancellery garden would have been nowhere near high enough to have achieved this effect. Either Baur misreported it, or this exchange never took place.

The Soviet interrogators were also made suspicious because Baur, despite weeping fits and depression, remained "far too calm" over all. They thought that Baur was a liar, a guilty liar, who was engaged in a "pretence".

Baur's unreliability was further undermined after he came out of captivity in the Soviet Union. When he had first been questioned, by Hugh Trevor-Roper, Baur had said that Martin Bormann had been killed in a tank explosion (although he confessed that he had not seen the body himself). But after he had met Artur Axmann he changed this story. Now he claimed that Bormann had not been killed in the tank explosion and that, on top of everything, he (Baur) had travelled with Bormann in certain further adventures.

To anyone familiar with criminal trials, Baur's profile is not unknown. He was, quite simply, a bad witness, unreliable and untrustworthy. It is not hard to see *why* he changed his testimony and although we are here dealing with a high moment in the history of the twentieth century, we should not accord Baur a bigger part than he was entitled to. Quite simply, at the crucial time when Hitler had shot himself, Baur was somewhere else.

SS Adjutant Otto Günsche's testimony has been criticised on three grounds: first, because it differs from Linge's; second, because he said that he sent a soldier to inspect the burning corpses on the evening of 30 April and the soldier had reported back that they had burned to nothing, when by common consent that couldn't have happened; and finally because he said that Axmann was present outside Hitler's suite in contradiction of Axmann's own claims (although Axmann did later change his version, to agree with Günsche).

The main point of disagreement between Günsche and the valet, Linge, was that Linge said he had seen a wisp of smoke under the map room door and had heard a single shot whereas Günsche had said the steel door to the *anteroom* was fireproof, gasproof and hence sound-proof, so no shot could have been heard.

When Günsche was interviewed by O'Donnell in the early 1970s, he reiterated the point that, while the group was waiting outside Hitler's suite, Linge was "really beside himself, running up and down those stairs like that." In such circumstances it is certainly easy to see why Linge may have confused the anteroom for the map room – they were next to each other. It is by no means unthinkable that he heard a shot – or thought he heard one when no one else did. In his disturbed state, he was highly suggestible. If that is what happened, then no amount of time in Soviet prisons would have had any effect; he would have re-membered what he remembered. Both the Russians and O'Donnell found Günsche a more impressive character than Linge.

It is also necessary to point out that so far as Trevor-Roper's book is concerned, we are relying not on the direct testimony of Linge but also on the secretaries who acted as intermediaries. In the speed of events in the last days, is it likely that one secretary got the news about Hitler's death from one particular man and the others from someone else, as Trevor-Roper reported? Rather, in the mêlée, everyone got their information from everyone else. The stories were mixed and rumour was joined to fact.

Now try to imagine the scene where Bormann, Goebbels and the others first enter Hitler's suite. There is the smell of cyanide and gun-shot. The situation cannot help but be ghoulish, macabre. Everyone is on edge, Linge especially. If we believe the later testimony of Linge and Günsche, there was undoubtedly a small hole near the right tem-ple of Hitler's head and blood trickled down. Who knows if, in the press of events, Linge at the very least didn't assume that this was an *exit* wound and concluded that the Führer must, therefore, have shot himself in the mouth. He could have spread this story in the Bunker where it was picked up by the secretaries, who in turn relayed it to Trevor-Roper during the course of his initial investigation. This would account for the discrepancy in which Günsche said Hitler shot himself in the head and Linge that he shot himself in the mouth.

What we do know now is that Günsche and Linge spent some years together in captivity in Russia where as we explained earlier; they were forced to write a book together about Hitler. Given that, one might have expected their stories to come together and to be all but identical by the time they were released. They did come to agree on the mode of death, a shot to the temple, but Linge still maintained he had heard a shot when Günsche and the others claimed they had not. This surely suggests a degree of honesty on their parts, rather than collusion. And what in fact changed in Linge's testimony was not whether Hitler shot himself in the mouth or temple, but that the mark on *der Chef's* temple changed from an *exit* wound to an *entry* wound. That is a far less serious discrepancy than it sounds, for how could a non-specialist be expected to know the difference? Yes, they could have concocted something but isn't it more likely that, cooped up together in Moscow for so long, Günsche finally convinced Linge that his version was correct?

Next, there is the testimony of Brigadeführer Johann Rattenhuber. His evidence added several extra facts of interest to the story. The account he wrote, which is still in the Russian KGB archives, says that on the morning of 30 April he accompanied Eva Braun up the steps of the Bunker to the garden, where she spent a few minutes. As we said earlier, just before the end she turned to Rattenhuber and said, "I just wanted to see the sun for the last time."

Like Axmann and Baur, Rattenhuber was a little the worse for wear from drink that afternoon, after the previous night's party in the canteen. When he arrived to be told that the Führer was dead, this head bodyguard actually lacked the courage to go into Hitler's living room and see for himself. He was still sitting on the beach outside in the corridor when Linge came out and placed both of Hitler's pistols on a shelf alongside Eva Braun's. Linge confirmed that Hitler was dead and then said he had just fulfilled, "the most difficult order that the Führer had given him". Rattenhuber quickly jumped to the conclusion that someone – presumably Linge – had given Hitler the *coup de grâce*.

Rattenhuber persisted in this belief for some time and for a while his Soviet interrogators shared his view, since it appears to have suited their opinion that Hitler had chosen the "coward's" way out. It certainly fuelled the idea among all those fascinated by Hitler's demise that someone had killed the Führer. Of course Linge's phrase could just as easily have applied to the fact that he had to enter Hitler's death room, then look after the disposal of the body. That, too, would be a very difficult duty to fulfil. After years in Soviet prisons, according to his written testimony, Rattenhuber himself came round to the view that this latter interpretation is what Linge had meant.

Finally, we examine an unusual piece of testimony from Harry Mengershausen. After his release from Russia, he described how, at the end of May 1945, he had been taken to a wood at Finow near Berlin and shown three: "charred and blackened corpses each lying in a wooden crate". Mengershausen said he had no difficulty identifying them: they were those of Hitler, Josef and Magda Goebbels. The Goebbels' corpses were only superficially burned, he said: but Hitler's, "was in a far worse state. The feet had been entirely consumed, the skin and flesh were blackened and burnt; but the facial structure remained clearly identifiable. There was a bullet hole in one temple, but the upper and lower jaw were both intact."

In other respects, Mengershausen was to prove a reliable witness, but in this case there are a number of serious inconsistencies in what he had to say. In the first place, the autopsy report said that the Hitler corpse had only one foot missing. Second, it said that: "on face and body the skin is completely missing; only remnants of charred muscle are preserved." Further on, it said: "the lower jawbone lies loose in the singed oral cavity." Finally, there was the apparent unequivocal comment: "part of the cranium is missing."

The files we have seen make no mention of Mengershausen's visit to Finow, though they do confirm that the corpses were held there for a while. It is difficult, therefore, to know what exactly to make of all this. If the Hitler corpse lacked its skin, as the autopsy report says, it would have been very difficult – impossible – for Mengershausen to identify the body as the Führer's. But then again would the Russians have placed another body there for some reason of their own? It seems unlikely, although it cannot be ruled out. And why did they not show him the corpse of Eva Braun? If he had identified her, surely that would have reinforced their certainty.

This testimony can be made to fit the other known facts *only* if Mengershausen was mistaken about the number of feet missing, did not notice that a small piece of skull was missing and, because of the bullet hole he saw, *assumed* the corpse was Hitler's. Lacking skin, it must have been unrecognisable. On this reasoning, it is possible – just – that the Hitler skull had *two* bullet holes, an entry wound and an exit wound. In other words, he shot himself in the temple and the bullet exited at the back of the skull.

We do not claim that this analysis completely solves the problems with the conflicting testimony of the various witnesses to Hitler's death. On the other hand, to return to the comparison to criminal trials – anyone who has had experience of such matters, as a lawyer or a police officer or on a jury, will know how, in almost any given case, there is conflicting eyewitness testimony. Sometimes that conflict is resolved, but often it is not. As countless psychological studies have shown, eyewitnesses are often absolutely certain of what they have seen even when it can be proved that they are wrong.

From our vantage point of having seen hitherto unpublished material from the Russian Operation Myth File, we now turn to the physical and forensic evidence. This may be divided into six parts: the finding of the bodies; the smell of bitter almonds; the dental evidence; the shrapnel wounds; rigor mortis; monorchism.

In the past there has been so much attention devoted to the dental evidence and the chemical evidence, that the physical nature of the evidence has been overlooked. And yet the physical evidence is what any policeman – the scene of crime officers – investigating this mystery would look at first. By physical evidence we mean the actual location of the bodies in the crater. This may seem a simple point but, like the psychological aspects considered above, it is fundamental.

So far as we can see, it has never been questioned that the bodies dug up in the crater were those burned. And the bodies *were* burned, albeit incompletely. We know from Trevor-Roper that the Russians found some 160 bodies in the garden of the Reichschancellery, which included quite a few that were jammed into the water tank. That was where the body of Hitler's double was found. None of the bodies in the tank was burned. We know that the Reichschancellery suffered from the heavy bombardment of Russian artillery, not to mention repeated Allied bombing. This undoubtedly claimed some lives. The shelling and the bombing no doubt created fires. And yet, the Operation Myth File is quite clear: *none* of the other 160 bodies in the Reichschancellery was burned, not one. In this one, crucial aspect Hitler's body, along with those of Braun and Josef and Magda Goebbels, was exceptional.

Nor is it likely that any of these other bodies would have been buried. Hitler's brother-in-law, Hermann Fegelein, was buried after his execution, but all witnesses concur in saying how dangerous it was even to go into the open to try to bury Hitler and Braun. When their corpses were set alight, everyone had to cower in the doorway to the Bunker because the shelling was so heavy. No one even tried to bury Josef and Magda Goebbels, no doubt due in part to the fact that the break-out was imminent and the survivors had other things on their mind. But again the shelling was heavy and this made burial dangerous. The Russians discovered the Goebbels' bodies where they had been left, on the open ground in front of the Bunker exit. If the Führer was buried in so perfunctory a way, would other corpses have been buried at all?

Nor should we forget that Harry Mengershausen, when asked by the Russians to indicate exactly where Hitler and Eva Braun had been buried, took his Soviet interrogators unprompted, "to the same crater in which Ivan Chiurakov had discovered the bodies." Incidentally, Ivan Klimenko, in our interview with him in 1995, told us something new about Mengershausen. This man had at first said that he had seen the burial of the Hitlers from the blue dining room, across the garden of the Chancellery, and therefore about 600 metres away. In fact, Mengershausen was one of the officers *who buried* Hitler and Braun. Klimenko says Mengershausen was afraid to admit this at first because the War was still going on and he felt he might be accused of being a member of Hitler's entourage. So this only adds to the credibility of his testimony in this regard.

And the Russians did discover *two* bodies in the crater, a man and a woman. What are the chances of other couples having been buried in this way? Not impossible, but extremely unlikely.

Harry Mengershausen had told the Russians that Hitler's dog Blondi had been buried in the same crater as the two bodies. This creature, he said, was an Alsatian with long ears, a black back and light flanks. A dog like this, along with the body of another, was also found in the crater.

Finally, in this matter of the corpses actually taken out of the Bunker and buried in the crater, let us address Hugh Thomas's contention that although the male corpse may have been Hitler, the female corpse was not Eva Braun. Here we have the testimony of Linge, Günsche, Kempka and Axmann inside the Bunker and of Erich Mansfeld, Hermann Karnau and Harry Mengershausen outside the Bunker. They all say they saw Eva Braun being carried through the Bunker and up the stairs to the Reichschancellery garden. Hilco Poppen's testimony is slightly different. He told James O'Donnell that, from a distance of 150 metres and using his binoculars, he could just make out the face of Eva Braun, though at the time he had no idea who she was. In other words, he saw a woman's head. But the fact that he couldn't recognise the face does not really matter. What matters is that the face of the female body was uncovered, for all to see. Hilco Poppen's testimony not only agrees with the others. If the woman's face had been left uncovered so that Goebbels could have seen it was not Eva Braun's, would he have gone ahead with the murder of his own children? No.

Now we may return to the point Hugh Thomas stresses, namely that the Soviet autopsy reports failed to mention the smell of bitter almonds during the dissection of the bodies of Hitler and Braun. To him, this is proof they were not poisoned.

If you remember, the autopsy report on Eva Braun was *not* silent regarding the smell of bitter almonds. The phrasing was different from the other autopsies, but the actual words "during autopsy a marked smell of bitter almonds" were used. And there were two other cases – Magda Goebbels and the small black dog – where there was no mention of the smell of bitter almonds and yet cyanide compounds were found in the internal organs. Looked at in this light, therefore, the (partial) failure to mention the smell of bitter almonds in the case of Hitler may not be as serious as it seems. Any clinician knows that circumstances vary from one case to another and the strength of the smell of bitter almonds may have varied greatly between one corpse and another.

Then did the autopsy fail to *find* cyanide compounds in the bodies of Hitler or Eva Braun or simply fail to *mention* it? Unlike the other corpses, no samples from the bodies of Hitler and Braun were sent for analysis. In all other cases – the Goebbels family, General Krebs, the dogs – this was done. The autopsies were each divided into four parts: an introduction, the external examination, the internal examination and a conclusion. Usually, at the end of the internal examination section, the report listed those items which had been "retained for testing". For example, in the case of General Krebs, a "glass jar with part of brain" was referred to the laboratory, plus "10cc of blood, in test tube". These listed objects were then sent "with no preservative added" to "Medical-Epidemiological Field Laboratory Number 291 [or 292]."

At first glance, this does look suspicious. But is it really? Here is Bezymenski's account of his conversation with Professor Dr Nikolai Alexandrovich Krayevski, one of the team of pathologists who carried out the autopsies. The interview took place in 1968 shortly before Bezymenski published his book. "Did you know whose corpses were being dissected?" Bezymenski asked. Krayevski replied: "As far as the Goebbels family and General Krebs were concerned, yes. About the two other corpses there was no precise information, but there was talk that they were probably Hitler and Eva Braun. I repeat, it was mere conjecture."

This is an important exchange for it shows that the purpose of the autopsies in the case of Hitler and Braun was different from the others. In the case of the Goebbels family and Krebs (and the dogs, for that matter), the pathologists' main concern was with the method of death. In the case of the other two corpses, the priority was with *identification*.

The actual form of the autopsy reports confirms this. In the case of Hitler and Eva Braun they concentrate more on the external examination than the internal examination, dwelling in each case on the teeth, as we wrote in Chapter 6. Unlike the other autopsy reports, they also give details of consultation with external authorities, such as the dental nurse Käthe Heusermann.

In other words, perhaps no traces of cyanide compounds were found in the corpses of Hitler and Braun simply because the autopsy team *did not look for them*. In addition, the autopsies took place on 8 May, the day the War in Europe ended. Who knows what other pressures the autopsy team were under as the War came to an end? Conceivably, like other people, they were celebrating the end of years of bitter hostilities. In his testimony to us, given in 1995, Ivan Klimenko confirmed that *he* at least did celebrate VE day at Göring's villa and that then, "the corpses were still sitting in our barn." Either way, the autopsy doctors were happy to assume that, if all the other corpses, including the dogs, had died by cyanide poisoning, so had Hitler and Braun.

In the case of both the small black dog and Magda and Josef Goebbels, all of whom were shot immediately after taking or being given cyanide, the compounds were identified in their internal organs. In other words, based on the picture revealed in the other autopsies, Hitler could have followed Professor Haase's recommended method of suicide – by taking a cyanide capsule and at the same time shooting himself.

We now return again to the dental evidence. According to Käthe Heusermann, supported by Fritz Echtmann, duplicate bridges were made for Hitler and Eva Braun in October 1944, even though Braun was supposed not to need any bridgework. Hitler, it seems, had much worse teeth, in fact only five of his teeth were his own and the rest were made up of three bridges, a large one in the upper jaw and two smaller ones in the lower jaw. So six bridges would have been made for Hitler, making eight bridges in all. According to Thomas' decoy theory, three bridges were fitted into Hitler's mouth, and the other three used to produce the false jaw that was left in the "decoy" corpse's mouth. One of Braun's bridges would have been used on her decoy corpse, thus leaving only one bridge in the box to be discovered by Russian troops when they visited the Chancellery dental office. In fact, Heusermann, who was taken there by the Russians, later gave conflicting testimony. At one point she said that only one bridge had been found, a duplicate for Eva. Elsewhere, she said that the Russians "also found a box of gold crowns and duplicate bridges for Hitler and Eva". One of these statements has to be wrong and if more than one bridge was found in the Chancellery office, the "forensic fraud" theory falls down. Our evidence from Fritz Echtmann, reported clearly in the Russian files, is that Echtmann provided the Russians with bridgework for *both* the Führer and his wife.

There is one other new piece of relevant evidence we can mention here. When we interviewed Ivan Klimenko in 1995, he recalled that Fritz Echtmann had said that he had made a special tooth for Eva Braun: "using some special technique. According to him, he never made such a tooth either before or after." If the Braun corpse had this tooth – and Klimenko insists that it did – this would seem very strong evidence. (It would also call into the question the very idea that Braun had near-perfect teeth.)

In fact, the evidence from the first Russian commission on which Dr Thomas bases his theories is nowhere near as conclusive as it might be. Vasili Gorbushin was the Counter Intelligence officer who was in charge of the investigation into whether the corpses found in the Chancellery garden were really those of Hitler and Braun. Bezymenski says he was told by Gorbushin that: "the dissecting doctors had taken into custody jawbones with many artificial bridges, crowns, and fillings." The context here does not make it clear whether all these were supposed to relate to Hitler and Braun, or to other patients who had used the Chancellery dental office. On the next page of Bezymenski's report, Gorbushin is quoted as saying that when he took Heusermann to the dental office what they actually found was: "X-ray photographs of the Führer's teeth and a few gold crowns that had been prepared." There was no mention of a box or of any bridges.

Then there is the question of the timing of this elaborate plan of deception. Dr Thomas concedes that it would necessarily have taken a while to plan and execute and, he believes, may even have been in operation as early as October 1944 when the bridges were made. His argument is that Eva Braun didn't need any bridgework and therefore the manufacture of two duplicate bridges for her shows that the plan went into effect at that early point. But is this sensible? It may have been clear by then that Germany was bound to lose the War and that, if it did, Hitler would commit suicide. But the Battle of the Bulge had still to take place, when the Germans very nearly reversed the tide of war, at least in the north. Werner Maser quotes Josef Kammhuber in his biography of Hitler. Hitler did not admit to himself, Kammhuber claims, that Germany would lose the War until the end of March 1945. In addition, for months everyone around Hitler assumed that if and when the end came, the final stand would take place in the south not in Berlin.

We know from almost all witnesses that the decision to remain in Berlin – and there seems to be no doubt about this – was not taken until the very end. It formed in Hitler's mind, as we have seen, after the catastrophic military news that brought about his nervous collapse on 22 April. Therefore, the plot – if plot there was – must have been concocted not in October 1944 but in the last week of April 1945. Given that, we must ask ourselves if the plan that Dr Thomas suggests could have been conceived and put into effect in that time. Possibly, the jaw could have been found and manufactured. Almost certainly, a fake Eva cadaver could have been found. But – and this is the crucial point – could Eva's agreement have been secured in so short a while?

One final point on the dental evidence. Hugh Thomas makes much of the fact that Hitler's jaw was found loose in the oral cavity. But that isn't quite true. It was actually found with the tongue gripped tightly between the upper and lower jaws. This entire arrangement may have been loose in the jaw but it was quite a structure to have forged, in that particular way.

It has to be said that, when these factors are taken into account, the Thomas scenario is, in our opinion, extremely unlikely. One might also ask whose plan this was? Eva's? Unlikely. If her motive was to escape death, she wouldn't have flown back to Berlin on 15 April. What other motive could she have? To marry Hitler and carry the flame of the Nazi movement herself? Again unlikely. In any case if she did escape, why didn't she do that? Would she have wanted to survive Hitler? She loved him and surely if she had known he was going to die and she was going to survive, she would have been distraught. Her serenity in the last days and the fact of her last-minute marriage to Hitler belie this scenario.

Most important in some ways is who *else* could have masterminded the plan? And if so, why? Thomas suggests the ss, but doesn't elaborate. Perhaps there were others who saw Eva Braun as a figure-head, but they did not include Goebbels or Borman, the two most powerful people in the Bunker. Perhaps there were people who felt sorry for her, who felt she didn't have to die. But if this is true, it is also true that this would have been an eleventh-hour plan concocted after she arrived in the Bunker on 15 April. In order to have set in train the processes whereby the false bridges were made, this plan would have had to deceive Hitler himself but not Linge, Günsche and others. This too seems extremely improbable. Braun was closest to Speer. He would surely have been central to any plan of this nature? Yet he wasn't even in the Bunker in the last days.

Thomas also makes much of a statement by Linge, that on the evening of 30 April – after the bodies had been burned – the valet went up to the Chancellery garden to look at the progress of the cremation. "Eva Braun's once trim figure had jack-knifed, under rigor mortis . . . she was now sitting upright as if riding in a saddle. Both arms were outstretched, and her hand seemed to be holding imaginary reins." Thomas is dismissive of this piece of testimony, very circumstantially vivid (and, to us, therefore smacking of authenticity) because, he said, the chemical necessary to cause rigor mortis is used up very rapidly after cyanide poisoning, so rigor is minimal.

Goebbels poisoned himself with cyanide as well as putting a bullet through his head. Yet the pictures of his corpse, published in this book, show his left arm jack-knifed at right-angles to the rest of his body. His fingers are curled as if they are holding imaginary reins. Here again we have the phenomenon known to every clinician, that people differ vastly in the way they respond to certain medical conditions and that text-book accounts of all manner of things very often do not conform at all closely to what is observed in real life. What happened to Goebbels shows that, despite what Thomas says about the interaction of cyanide and rigor mortis being true, Linge's testimony about Eva Braun could also be true.

Hugh Thomas was first alerted to the fraud hypothesis by the fact that the corpse of Braun had suffered shrapnel wounds which had caused a haemorrhage in the lungs. This could not have happened to a dead body, he says, therefore the woman must have been killed by shrapnel and could not have been Eva. Thomas has more of a case here, but is his interpretation the only one? Remember always that the Soviet autopsy report on Eva's body included the words "during autopsy a marked smell of bitter almonds". Remember also that the Hitler corpse was missing a foot and that part of its cranium was missing, as were parts of the cranium and frontal cranium of the Braun body. Remember too that Semenovsky's commission reported that the bomb crater where the bodies were found showed some discolouration due to the presence of shrapnel. Remember, finally, that the party of people which attended the burning of the corpses was forced to shelter in the doorway of the emergency exit to the Bunker, at least to begin with, because Russian shelling was so heavy. Is all this not consistent with the corpses being hit by shrapnel soon after they were moved into the Reichschancellery garden and while they were burning? When it was time for burial, one of the soldiers searched in vain for a flag for a shroud. There was a blanket over Hitler but Braun was uncovered and unprotected.

Dr Thomas says that the haemorrhage in the lungs could only have been produced in a *live* person because only then would there be sufficient pressure in the arteries to force the blood into those cavities. But neither he nor anyone outside the Buch autopsy clinic ever saw the haemorrhages. Perhaps, in this case, the shrapnel themselves provided their own pressure in hitting the body? After all, at that point Braun had been dead for no more than an hour or so, if that.

We cannot know that this is what happened and offer it only as a theory. But other circumstances point so strongly to the corpse being Eva Braun that some cohesive argument of this kind is needed, to account for all the facts.

At this point, we finally need to consider the question of Hitler's monorchism, or alleged monorchism. Bezymenski said in his *The Death of Adolf Hitler* that this defect of Hitler's "had not been mentioned anywhere in the existing literature" and moreover that Professor Hans Karl von Hasselbach, one of Hitler's physicians, remembered that the Führer always refused categorically to have a medical check-up. Bezymenski quoted a book on Hitler's health, published in 1966, as supporting evidence of this. However, he was firmly contradicted by Werner Maser in his 1973 biography, who said that Dr Erwin Giesing (an ear, nose and throat specialist), had examined the Führer in July and October 1944 and examined his penis and testicles, writing afterwards that: "So far as I could see, the genitals ... showed no abnormalities." Dr Theo Morell also told Baur that: "so far as his sexual organs were concerned [Hitler] was completely normal."

Morell's testimony, it should be said, may not be worth much. He was a venereal specialist who first examined Hitler for syphilis. The results of this test were never released and were missing from Hitler's records which were published in 1981. Morell has also been described as a "degenerate" figure, obsessed with money, who used to push his own brand of drugs that were manufactured in Budapest. His notes, according to another doctor, revealed a "total ignorance of medicine", and "a total lack of proper investigative technique". Morell was obsessed with keeping his position with Hitler and keeping other medical men at bay. He therefore had a vested interest in making out that Hitler was normal in any area where he was not himself a specialist. There was also a risk in admitting to anyone that Hitler was abnormal in a sexual sense. If that rumor had got about in the very macho Nazi hierarchy – and if Hitler found that Morell was the source of the story – he would have been out on his ear and very possibly worse. In any case, after the War, Morell told American investigators that he did not: "have any knowledge of his Führer below the waist." Morell was no more reliable than Baur.

Dr Giesing was a better doctor, a more thorough investigator, as his records show, and in fact this may explain the apparent discrepancy. "I . . . drew the bedclothes right back to uncover the lower parts of his body . . . So far as I could *see*, the genitals . . . showed no abnormalities." The italics – added by us – stress the fact that the meticulous Dr Giesing did not actually feel Hitler's testicles, but just cast his eyes over the Führer's body. And although Giesing later told Maser in conversation in 1971 that Hitler's testicles were "normal and unimpaired", that was not his wording in June 1945 when he wrote his initial deposition on Hitler for the Allies.   Suffice to say that monorchism is a fairly frequent phenomenon and does not affect sexual activity. Hitler may have *appeared* normal to his doctors but he may only have ever had his genital organs *looked at* by medical men, not examined more closely. Therefore, his defect would have only become truly apparent when his scrotum was dissected in the autopsy.

Finally, we were given a new piece of medical evidence by Ivan Klimenko in 1995. After telling us not to be too fazed by the way witnesses changed their stories – reminding us that they were all worried about their own fate as the War was still raging – Klimenko said that they found the earth very "crumbly" when digging the crater. He then added that the body they found there had been confirmed as Hitler's because, "as is known, Hitler was wounded during World War One." The Russians found confirmation of this wound on the corpse.

In fact, Hitler suffered three wounds during his life. In a World War One he was wounded in the left thigh which, according to John Toland in his book on Hitler, left him with a: "bean-size oval-shaped deeply furrowed scar (with its longitudinal axis running from bottom to top) above the middle of the exterior." Hitler never knew if there were any shell splinters left in it. He was also gassed in 1918, actually finishing that War in hospital. On top of that, during the Munich (Beer Hall) Putsch attempt in November 1923 he had fallen heavily and injured his left collarbone and upper arm (his arm was paralysed for some time). He'd also sustained a bruised right arm and pierced eardrums during the assassination attempt of July 1944, known as the Generals' Plot. Klimenko meant that thickening on both bones – thigh and collar bone – were visible (though it has to be said that these were *not* mentioned in the autopsy reports).

After these six distinct areas of physical evidence, we now need to turn to the final matter, namely the remains of the skull which were found by the second Russian commission. There are four fragments, two larger pieces, one with an exit wound formed by a bullet, and two smaller pieces. From the television documentary film made by Ada Petrova, these pieces appear to fit together.

In *Doppelgänger*, Dr Thomas admits he was denied access to the skull remains. While sympathising, this in itself cannot be counted as proof that the Russians were hiding evidence. We, on the other hand, have been allowed access. After her first visit to Bolshaya Pirogovskaya Street – and after filming the skull and archive – Ada Petrova returned a second time with Professor Zyagin, an independent expert. He handled the skull, measured it, photographed it, probed the edges and the bullet hole itself.

Nor need we pay undue attention to Dr Thomas' reservations that the skull was stored in Moscow in a cardboard box of very thin material. As Ada's film evidence makes clear, despite this apparently flimsy protection the skull was kept in the State Archive of the Russian Federation under wax seal. It was adequately preserved.

Dr Thomas has reservations about the skull fragments themselves. But we have seen the commission report at first hand, which says that: "the shot was fired either in the mouth or the right temple at point blank range."

Thomas also notes that some of the interlocking bone junctions are seen to be undone but still intact, suggesting that "the bone was artificially removed from a skull and did not come adrift in any fire." In other words, this too was a piece of forensic faking. The suture lines, the edges of the bone where they are knitted together, are in fact stronger than the bones themselves, he says, and therefore should not have come apart before the bones.

Thomas has at least six other points to make about the skull bones: first, that the shape of the hole formed in the piece of skull in the Moscow archive was "likely" to have been caused by faking, by a bullet which passed more or less *straight* through the skull (our italics) rather than at any angle, as would have happened in any suicide attempt; second, that the burning of the skull would not have produced remnants of this nature; third, that even if the skull was real, the damage it showed could only have been sustained if the bullet had been fired either from the left front parietal area (the left side of the forehead) or a shot in the mouth, with the bullet being deflected by the sphenoid bone, all areas which were found intact by Soviet pathologists; fourth, the bone (broadcast fleetingly on Russian television) showed very little evidence of sustained fire damage; fifth, the edges of the sutures suggest a much younger man than Hitler's fifty-six years; and, finally, that the skull fragment on its underside was not scored by venous sinuses, which normally give a skull of this kind a "hot-cross bun" appearance, calling into question whether it was an occipital fragment at all.

Each of these may or may not be a telling point. They are telling if, as Hugh Thomas claims, the Russian investigators were anxious to please Stalin and would do anything to give him the result they thought he wanted. If the Russians faked the evidence, then clearly any speculation, or inference, or deduction, about the last days of Hitler, using this skull as evidence, is pointless. Thomas himself refers to the Russian reports as saying that the discovery of the skull fragments in 1946 was "miraculous", implying that everything had been arranged to order.

Perhaps.

But if the discovery was real, it would have had to take place in exactly the location it *was* found. Far from being miraculous, it would have been obvious and prosaic.

So Dr Thomas' litany of doubts is nowhere near as damning as it seems *unless* the Russians faked their evidence. How likely is that? Quite frankly, it is impossible to give an answer. All we know is that the investigation of the skull (and its discovery) was carried out in 1946 and not released until now, 1995. Not even Bezymenski was told about it. The photographic evidence in the file is mounted on blue card with captions carefully written in boxes with arrows pointing to the important areas. If all this is fake, it was done a long time ago.

Can anything be read into the fact that Bezymenski was kept in the dark? One possibility is that the skull evidence conflicted with the poisoning evidence. It seems the Russians were intent on proving that Hitler took the "coward's" way out and poisoned himself at the time. It may also be that they doubted the findings of the second commission. At this stage, fifty years after the event, it is impossible to say.

At the end of the day, if we assume that the Russians did not fake any evidence – and if we allow ourselves not to be prejudiced by all the detail of the so-called forensic fakes, all of which is in some way flawed – and if instead we concentrate on the important aspects of the chain of events in the Bunker in the last days as well as on the psychological background and the apparently well-attested confirmation of where the bodies were buried and dug up, we arrive at an accurate conclusion: that Adolf Hitler and Eva Braun *did* die as Hugh Trevor-Roper said they did, with Hitler taking poison and then shooting himself and with Eva Braun taking poison. We may also conclude that they were taken out of the Bunker near the emergency exit, incompletely burned, buried in a shell crater, dug up by Russian troops and correctly identified by means of their teethwork. Moreover, a year later, remains of Hitler's skull were dug up from the same crater in the Reichschancellery garden, proving conclusively that Hitler *was* shot through the head. It is impossible to say whether he shot himself in the mouth or through the temple, but in other words the skull in Moscow *is* Hitler's.

We have tried to adopt a commonsense approach, following this fifty-year-old detective trail from Berlin to Moscow. We have treated the evidence as a policeman would, rather than trying to create sensation for the sake of it.

But we offer one final proof. Since doubt has been cast on the authenticity of the skull in Moscow, we asked for permission to have an independent medical expert examine it. Surprisingly, this permission was granted and, as we have said earlier in this chapter, we commissioned Professor Viktor Zyagin from the Federal Centre of Medical Forensic Examination (the same institute as Pyotr Semenovsky).

Zyagin said he was eighty per cent sure that the skull was Hitler's. His doubts were those of a scientist, who rarely claims to be certain of anything. His specific findings were as follows:

- the bones are the back of the parietal and part of the occipital bone;
- the hole is in the parietal area and the shot was made from below, maybe in the mouth, maybe in the chin; (This solves one problem, which has confused many people – namely, how could

Hitler have shot himself *and* bitten into the ampoule when he had a gun in his mouth? The barrel of the Walther would surely have impeded any biting action? But by shooting himself through the underside of the chin, Hitler would have been able to place the ampoule in his mouth, prepare himself and then bite through the glass of the Zyankali capsule only moments before he squeezed the trigger. Whether or not it happened, it makes sense.)

- the fragments are burned at the edges;
- the skull comes from an adult; the conclusion was based on an analysis of the sutures;
- the age of the person was in the forty-five to fifty-five range; (Hitler, of course had jsut celebrated his fifty-sixth birthday ten days before his death.)
- the person suffered severe headaches: "There are widespread finger-made depressions indicating inner cranial pressure, as if this person is suffering from persistent headaches."
- judging by the colour of the skull fragments, the person was a vegetarian. Normally, said Professor Zyagin, the skull colour is yellow, but in the case of this skull it is grey-blue. (Hitler, of course, had his own vegetarian cook in the Bunker, Fräulein Konstanze Manzialy.)

Part II

Hitler's Other Remains

8

THE SPY IN THE BUNKER

The documentary and other material relating to the Führer, which Ada Petrova discovered in the secret Russian archives, throws light on several different aspects of both Hitler's last days and his character. Although not strictly related to our narrative, the clues they provide to Hitler the man are too important to pass over. The first of these relates to the issue of whether or not there was a spy inside the Bunker.

This was a subject of endless fascination and concern to Hitler himself. He was, it is fair to say, a somewhat paranoid individual. After his discovery of the highly successful *Rote Kapelle* communist espionage ring, uncovered by the RHSA (Himmler's secret service), and of the Stauffenberg conspiracy (the Generals' Plot) to assassinate him in July 1944, he had good reason.

But that there might have been a spy inside the Bunker of the Reichschancellery itself in the last days was not considered in the immediate aftermath of the War. For a start, many accounts of the Battle of Berlin have echoed Cornelius Ryan's opinion voiced in *The Last Battle*: "Although the Russians knew that the FührerBunker lay beneath the Reichskanzlei, it took them several hours to find it. People were grabbed off the streets and asked to direct the searchers to the place. Gerhard Menzel, a photographer, was one who was asked. He had never heard of the Bunker. Still, he went with one group of soldiers to the wrecked Reichskanzlei. In the labyrinth of cellars and passageways Russian engineers led the way with mine detectors. As soon as a room or corridor was cleared, other soldiers collected papers, files and maps. Menzel was suddenly given a pair of binoculars the Russians had found and told to leave. They had arrived at the FührerBunker itself."

This sort of account does suggest that the Russians had no idea where the Bunker was and were by no means certain what went on inside.

After the War, however, it was revealed gradually that Hitler had been seriously worried in the last weeks, months even, about a security leak from his headquarters. James O'Donnell first heard it from Minister for Armaments, Albert Speer. "In that last fortnight, when Hitler mentioned *das Leck* [the leak] he knew what he was talking about, a steady flow of information out of the Bunker. For example," Speer is quoted in *The Berlin Bunker*, "he told me of an order a couple of months back – I believe it was a rather routine promotion list – that he had for some reason pulled back and *not* sent to the OKW [Armed Forces High Command] or the OKH [Army High Command]. Yet within forty-eight hours, he complained, the news of these 'promotions' was on the British radio . . . During my last visit to the FührerBunker on 23/24 April I recall Hitler mentioning that he had at last called in both Ernst Kaltenbrunner of the RSHA and Gestapo Chief Heinrich Mueller to make a thorough probe of Bunker internal security."

Hitler's private pilot Baur agreed with Speer that Hitler was obsessed with *das Leck* and the telephone operator Rochus Misch said that, during the last fortnight, Hitler would sometimes ask: "Misch, what do you think of so-and-so? Can we be sure he is secure?"

One of the reasons for this suspicion about a leak was a secret pirate radio station supposedly operated by the SS but in reality a propaganda play perpetrated by the British. This was *Soldatensender* Calais. It had begun in 1943 and was beamed by shortwave from England, its "Calais" dateline specifically chosen to confuse German Army direction-finding devices. The programmes broadcast were very clever. They were mainly traditional military tunes and *Wehrmacht* bulletins, into which were inserted high-level gossip about the goings-on in Hitler's headquarters. Jokes were made at the expense of the British, Americans and Russians but, in among all this, the audience was slowly given the message that they were being led by a bunch of sharks who were enjoying themselves while others fought and died for their country. This diet of Bunker gossip, enough of which was accurate, made the programme very popular. Even soldiers stationed in and around the Reichschancellery Bunker network itself confessed later that they had tuned in.

The leak had been going on for more than a year by the time Hitler was confined to the Bunker, but it was only by April 1945 that he became truly concerned. O'Donnell felt that he had the answer. He was sure that it was mixed up with the Fegelein affair. Hermann Fegelein, it will be remembered, was the man who had married Eva Braun's sister and was Himmler's ambassador at Hitler's HQ. According to Hugh Trevor-Roper, Fegelein had decided he wanted to escape the Bunker.

But once his absence was noticed, he was run to ground and forcibly brought back. After news of Himmler's attempt to negotiate a surrender with the Western Allies reached the Führer, Fegelein was stripped of his rank and subsequently shot as an accessory.

In *The Berlin Bunker*, O'Donnell believed that there was more to it than that. For about a year, he says, Fegelein had been keeping a very attractive mistress in a rambling apartment house in the Charlottenburg area of Berlin, just off the fashionable Kurfuerstendamm. Günsche, Baur, Mohnke and Misch all met the lady in question. O'Donnell believes that she was a spy. He says that when Fegelein had been arrested in the Charlottenburg apartment, a valise was taken at the same time. When this was examined, in the presence of Bormann, besides money and jewels and three gold watches, two passports were found, in different names but both showing the photograph of this woman. One of the passports was British. Bormann, "roaring like a wounded bull," pounded the table with both fists and exploded that his men had not captured her too. "Fegelein is a traitor," he screamed. "This woman is British, an enemy agent. Fegelein went to bed with this spy and blabbered everything. *She* was *das Leck*."

The Russian evidence tells a rather different story.

In 1945, Ivan Paderin was the Deputy Commander in charge of political affairs of the regiment that was storming the Reichschancellery. This was 220th regiment of the 79th division. Ada Petrova tracked him down after finding his name in the documents. Paderin reports that, on 21 April 1945, his unit – part of the 8th Guards Army – reached the south-eastern suburbs of Berlin.

The Russian tactics were to use small "storming units", the same approach that had been developed in the battle of Stalingrad in 1943. (Paderin himself had been at Stalingrad.) During the day, the Russians would study exactly where the German defences were located and then at night, using artillery barrages to begin with, they would attack those defences.

The battle on 21 April was very hard: 2000 American and British bombers had laid the area in ruins but German resistance was tough and the Russians were forced to make advances where they could. "We were like miners," said Paderin, "hacking our way through walls to make progress. It was impossible to be on the open street. Not only were they filled with rubble, but they were under devastating fire.

"On 29 April we reached the Landwehr Canal which was the last line [of defence] before the Tiergarten. The Reichschancellery was about 400 metres beyond this canal. It was a huge stone building, with enormous columns. There were two storeys above the ground and, we knew, two storeys below ground. On the opposite side of the canal we were faced by units known as Leibstandarten Adolf Hitler. Their defence was a fierce one and they held us up for almost a day. To test the strength of the German forces, we threw dummies into the canal. We clothed the dummies in the uniforms of our own colleagues who had been killed. Always, the dummies were ripped apart by gunfire as soon as they hit the waters of the canal.

"After a day the wind changed and began to flow in the direction of the Reichschancellery. In our unit we had chemical warfare specialists and we now set up a smokescreen. Smoke poured from every can and covered everything. Just where we were holding there was a tram bridge on the left and a different bridge on the right. Our aim was to blanket the bridges in smoke, so that we could cross the canal. Before we made a move, our flame throwers started up. Now the Leibstandarten stopped their resistance and withdrew in the direction of the Reichschancellery. Thus we managed to cross the canal.

"At about 1 o'clock, my radio officer caught a signal from the German radio station. The text of this signal ran as follows: 'Russians, please stop your fire. We are sending a parliamentarian to the tram bridge.' From the headquarters of our army there came an order to hold our fire. After the immense barrage that had gone before, there then followed such a silence that there was ringing in my soldiers' ears.

"Suddenly, I heard a very unpleasant sound right beneath my feet, a series of disgusting squeals. It was a huge pack of big black cockroaches which was streaming towards the canal. They were deserting Hitler, making use of the silence!

"Although I was formally second-in-command in my unit, at that time my commanding officer was in the hospital, injured, and so I was in fact in charge. I sent some of my men to the observation posts to monitor the Reichschancellery. I myself found a hole in a wall from where I could see the headquarters building. From there I saw three persons make their exit from the southern wing of the chancellery. One of these was the commander of the German groundforces, General Krebs. He was accompanied by two soldiers who had white pieces of cloth attached to their bayonets. They came up to the bridge and at that point they were met by our Intelligence officers. They asked for a message to be passed on to General Chuikov and Marshal Zhukov on the conditions of ceasefire. The negotiations continued throughout the night of 30 April-1 May and throughout the next day.

"Our soldiers established a telephone line between Russian head-quarters and the Imperial Reichschancellery. The Germans were asking us to telephone Grand-Admiral Dönitz, who was Hitler's successor as Führer, for only with his help could the fate of Germany's future be resolved. Dönitz, we were told, was in Mecklenberg. Zhukov, of course, insisted on unconditional surrender. We heard everything on the radio. We were doing nothing at this time. Some of us were resting, others were just watching the cockroaches."

Paderin continued his reminiscences, prompted by Ada Petrova. "For the storming of the Reichschancellery, our Intelligence officers were given a special briefing on Hitler. We were told his age, his physical appearance, his height, the fact that his left arm wasn't functioning properly etcetera, the fact that he had a small black moustache. All the soldiers read these details with great interest because, in his heart, every soldier wanted to be the man to seize Hitler and bring him before Stalin alive. This very desire, to seize Hitler alive, was pushing us forward, although I emphasised to my men that these were the last days of the War and they should not risk their lives unnecessarily.

"The negotiations with Krebs lasted thirteen hours and although Goebbels offered to make a broadcast, agreement could not be reached and Krebs and the soldiers were returned to the Chancellery. Then the final storming of the building began.

"To tell the truth it was an anti-climax because my unit entered the southern wing of the Chancellery without a fight. The garden of the Reichschancellery was a complete mess. People were zig-zagging all over the place, running this way and that. For some reason there were a lot of Germans in monastic garb. Where were they going? Who were *they* deserting?

"Already our cooks were setting up their field kitchens in the Reichschancellery, and preparing typical Russian *kasha* (a kind of porridge). However, our troops were very strained by now and weren't hungry. They didn't even feel the need to drink alcohol. An Intelligence officer in those first moments told me that Hitler's chauffeur, Kempka, had bought some gasoline to burn Hitler's corpse. I went down into the cellar in the Bunker, to the third floor. The first thing I saw was the burnt corpse of Goebbels, his wife and their children. Krebs, the man who had tried to negotiate the ceasefire with Zhukov, was also there. I thought he had shot himself. His body was lying there, besides a table.

Bormann wasn't there and our Intelligence officers were already at work in the Bunker. Other Intelligence officers had already found Hitler's corpse in the bomb crater and pulled it free, into the garden.

"I looked down at the charred corpse. He was lying with one side of his body badly burned, especially his arm and leg and face – it was impossible to identify him by the face. But the identification procedure started. All around, at the time, I could hear one pistol shot after another. Only gradually did I understand that these sounds meant that members of Hitler's entourage were still committing suicide.

"Approximately forty people were ushered out of the Reichschancellery – they had not managed to commit suicide. They were supposed to identify Hitler. They formed a line and they were brought to the corpse, one by one. As they were led forward, one at a time, they would suddenly call out, at a distance of perhaps twenty metres, '*Ja! Ja! Das ist der Führer.*' Then, when they got closer, they would change. 'No,' they would say. 'That isn't Hitler.' Thus, even after we had questioned forty persons, it wasn't clear whether the corpse was Hitler or not.

"The rumour emerged that there were doubles. One was found in the street nearby and another inside the Reichschancellery. I saw both of them.

"I was unsure myself whether the corpse was Hitler or not. We obtained Hitler's medical records – which had been completed with the usual German meticulousness – and we made some measurements, such as the length of the fingers. From this it seemed that we were dealing with the genuine Hitler's corpse. Apparently, Hitler put an ampoule into his mouth and bit it but, due to the fact that he was a vegetarian, this poison didn't kill him. But he began suffering from enormous pain and began crying and shouting. When one of his Adjutants heard these screams, he entered into the room and shot Hitler in the mouth. That is why he has this outgoing bullet hole somewhere near the forehead or temple.

"At that time Ivan Serov, who was head of the Front Counter-Intelligence, arrived at the Reichschancellery. When he arrived, all the people who were gathered around the corpse were pushed to one side and the special services started their work. I didn't see where, in what direction, Hitler's corpse was carried away.

"I went down into the Bunker again. Everything was destroyed and the electricity generator had been blown out. I only had my army light and it wasn't possible to see anything there. My soldiers were very upset at not being able to seize Hitler alive. They had missed a great opportunity.

"In my unit there was an Intelligence officer, Ivan Purov, an extremely brave man. All of a sudden Purov brought a man, a German Major, who had the uniform of a civilian telegraphist. I started to yell at him. 'Why on earth are you bringing me a civilian when there is a war going on?' He replied: 'Please, major, don't yell at me. Search him and then we'll have a talk.' Actually, in the tunic of this civilian telegraphist, there were secret documents. Two of these documents I can cite even now [in 1994] because I remember them by heart. 'I am leaving you with a woman, who came to me in the completely surrounded city, lest she see the disgrace of Germany. My last wish and my order to my deputy, Martin Bormann, is to pass all my assets to the Party. If there is no Party, then to the State. I also ask that my relatives are not forgotten, especially Frau Winter, who worked for me for more than twenty years. [She was his secretary/stenographer, who spoke fluent Russian.] The thing should be done in such a way that there is no trace left of my ashes.' This document was dated 4 pm, 29 April 1945 and signed. The witnesses were Goebbels, Bormann and Krebs.

"The second document was an organisational document. 'Before my death, I expel from the party Göring and Himmler because they are holding negotiations behind my back . . .' ."

This was a copy of the documents – the Will and Political Testament – mentioned in Hugh Trevor-Roper's reports.

"I believe that Ivan Serov organised the transfer of Hitler's corpse to Moscow. Later, I held Hitler's skull in the Krasnogorsk archive [see Appendix B]. I had got to know Serov quite well after an encounter at the end of the War when his men tried to turf my men out of a billet they had. Smersh had a lot of power but we managed to keep our billet. After that, I think Serov had a certain respect for me, that I would stand up for my men, even against Smersh. At one point, I was contemplating writing a book about my experiences and at that time Serov was head of the KGB. I approached him and he gave me a special pass for access to the Krasnogorsk archive. There was a document attached to the bones saying that this was the skull of Hitler and that this was the result of an examination. I had to give the paper back as soon as I had read it and do not remember who signed this document.

"I now want to tell you about Alexander Kvapishevski, Sasha Kvap, as he was known. He was a hero of the Soviet Union and has been here in this apartment of mine three times. He died in the 1960s, a strange death because blood blocked his throat.

"I believe that Kvap became Hitler's messenger in the Bunker, having been recruited through the Gestapo. Hitler's Adjutants would bring top secret documents to Kvap whose responsibility it was to take them to Zossen." Zossen, code-named *Maybach I*, was the headquarters of OKH (Army High Command), headed by General Guderian. A mile away was a completely separate encampment, *Maybach II*, the headquarters of OKW (Armed Forces High Command). Zossen was heavily bombed by the Americans on 15 March 1945, at the request of the Russians, according to author Cornelius Ryan. The message from Marshal Sergei V. Khudyakov of the Red Army General Staff, to General John R. Deane, Chief of the US Military Mission in Moscow, now on file in Washington and Moscow – and appearing here for the first time – is an astonishing document for the insight it offers into the extent of Russian intelligence in Germany: 'Dear General Deane, according to information we have, the General Staff of the German Army is situated thirty-eight kms south of Berlin, in a specially fortified underground shelter called by the Germans "The Citadel." It is located ... five-and-a-half to six km south-south-east of Zossen and one to one-and-a-half km east of a wide highway ... which runs parallel to the railroad from Berlin to Dresden. The area occupied by the underground fortifications ... covers about five to six km. The whole area is surrounded by wired entanglements several rows in depth, and is very strongly guarded by an SS regiment. According to the same source the construction of the underground fortification was started in 1936 ... Enclosed is a map with the exact location of the German General Staff [headquarters].'"

"Kvap," Paderin told Petrova in 1994, "had the necessary equipment to copy the documents which he carried between Berlin and Zossen. Our Command knew about the contents of these secret documents very quickly, almost immediately. It was Kvap who told me the story about how the cyanide didn't kill Hitler because he was a vegetarian, and that one of his aides had shot him.

"For the final assault on Berlin all the political officers were summoned by the Counter Intelligence Service, Smersh. We were told that on German territory we might come across Russian Intelligence officers in German uniforms. We were told they might come up to us and utter a password which was *Vitkof* (or *Kvitkof*). It appears to be a codeword rather than a word with a meaning. In such an eventuality, the political officers were told, it was their responsibility to provide security for these double agents.

"When I was in Berlin I met Sasha Kvap. In the garden of the Reich-schancellery, a person in a German military uniform, with the rank of Captain, came up to me. He came up to me, cursing in fluent Russian, and he uttered this password – *Kvitkof*. He told me that the most secret documents were disappearing [destroyed] and added: 'We need a car to save them and to ship them to the proper place. I said that of course we had a car, but then I asked him how he could travel around Berlin in a German uniform – he would be immediately killed. I therefore gave him my long raincoat and personally put the coat on his shoulders. After that moment I didn't see him for many, many years. Then I ran into him in 1954."

Another witness traced by Ada Petrova was Lieutenant-Colonel Veniamin Mindlin, Commander of the 1st Guards Armour Brigade, who just happened to be following Serov's car as it approached the Reichschancellery. Mindlin, who later became Commander of a Division, says that he saw a man being escorted out of the Chancellery with a bag, a sort of sack, over his head. Other officers thought that this might be Bormann but Mindlin asked Serov who it was. Serov replied that it was none of Mindlin's business and that unless he wanted to be "turned into camp dust" he had better forget what he had seen. Mindlin now believes that he witnessed Kvap – who has become something of a legend in Russian Intelligence circles – being hustled away to safety.

Paderin's and Mindlin's eyewitness testimony was confirmed by a third source, Sergei Kondrashov, who was an Intelligence officer during the War and is now a Lieutenant-General of the Russian External Intelligence Service, formerly the First Chief Directorate of the KGB. "Everything that was happening in Hitler's Bunker was known to us," he said. "We knew every day, every minute, every second, what was happening there. Today people are disputing a trifle. Either Hitler put an ampoule of cyanide in his mouth, bit it, and then shot himself, or he put an ampoule in his mouth and someone else shot him. The issue of Hitler's death is complex but it was investigated several times chiefly because Stalin hoped to have Hitler alive. It's really hard to say what Stalin would have done with Hitler if he had captured him alive, because Stalin's own actions were always unpredictable."

Although Sacha Kvap died in the 1960s, his wife is still alive and living in Russia. As this book went to press, efforts were still being made by us to contact her. The information released so far is clearly unsatisfactory. If Kvap is the mole, one would like to know for example exactly how he was recruited, what his German name was, who his Russian contacts were and how these communications were carried out.

But that there was an Allied spy very close to Hitler in those final weeks – and that it was a Russian man not a British woman – now seems beyond doubt. In addition to the O'Donnell and Cornelius Ryan evidence, many on the Allied side thought that either ss General Heinrich Müller or Martin Bormann himself was the spy. Müller was fingered because Mohnke prepared a list of people close to Hitler in the last days, for the Russians, from which Müller's name was omitted. As it became clear that Müller *had* been close to the Führer, the suspicion naturally arose that the Russians had excluded from this list one of their own operatives. Bormann was suspected by Werner Naumann, Goebbels' deputy, who told the Allies that Bormann had escaped the Bunker and gone straight to Russian military headquarters, "because he had always been a Soviet spy". This theory, it has to be said, fits with Paderin thinking the man with the bag over his head was Kvap and Kondrashov thinking it was Bormann. It might also fit with Stalin saying, in the late summer of 1945, first that Hitler and then Bormann had escaped in the submarine that left Hamburg in the last days of the War, a subtle piece of disinformation to put the Allies off the track. But this is to allow speculation to go too far. According to other Intelligence sources, who analysed what was leaked, the Russian agent in the Bunker: "was not clever at interpreting political events but . . . did know a great deal in detail about most of Hitler's activities." This appeared to be confirmed by the wrangle between the Allies over Germany's production and strength of u-boats at the very end of the War. British and American naval Intelligence told the Russians that a new type of u-boat, with a range of 31,500 miles at ten knots, did not exist. Yet the Russians, through their spy, already had the registration numbers of a hundred of these submarines. They could take this information no further, however, an indication, according to William Stevenson in his book *The Bormann Brotherhood*: "that their highly placed spy at Nazi Party headquarters was someone with an overall view of confidential matters but without sufficient detailed knowledge to pursue inquiries into specific areas. He was good at passing over bulk material but lacked either the time or the expertise to evaluate all of it." Unless it was a deliberate deception, surely this would seem to rule out Bormann or Naumann?

We made enquiries about Kvap at the Department of External Intelligence in Moscow (the former KGB), but were fobbed off. "Such a person did not exist," we were told. However, what Paderin did tell us was that Kvap had at first worked in the Gestapo before coming under the wing of Rudolf Schmundt.

Schmundt was Hitler's Chief Adjutant and had been since 1938. He was thus very close to the Führer and went everywhere with him, arranged many of his appointments and, to an extent, had control over how much time people spent with Hitler. He was one of the Führer's greatest admirers and, on occasion, would reprimand other officers for not showing sufficient loyalty or not acknowledging Hitler's "greatness". This sycophancy paid off. Between 1938 and 1944 he rose from the rank of Major to that of Lieutenant-General and was appointed Chief of the Army Personnel Office in 1943. Thereafter all appointments to Army posts were made by Hitler personally, through Schmundt.

Schmundt was seated just five chairs from Hitler, at the end of the table, on 20 July 1944 when, at 12.30 pm, an explosion rocked the *Lagebaracke* in the Wolf's Lair. The attempt on Hitler's life – the Generals' Plot – killed four senior officers, Schmundt among them. That day he lost a leg and died forty-eight hours later. As a measure of Hitler's feeling for his Adjutant, he told Schmundt's widow not to expect him to support her: "You must console me," he said.

Schmundt was replaced by General Wilhelm Burgdorf. Like Schmundt, he had total access to the Führer and even if they weren't as close in personal terms, from the Russians' point of view, they still had a man close to the centre of power. Moreover, in the final days, Burgdorf shared a room in the Bunker with Krebs, by then Head of OKW (Army High Command) and in charge of the fighting on the eastern front.

A Captain on Schmundt's and Burgdorf's staff, who acted as a courier between the Bunker and Zossen, as Paderin told us, certainly fits with the pattern of Intelligence which was supplied. That is, its quality was good but analysis was absent. Neither Schmundt nor Burgdorf, as Adjutants, were in a position to probe behind the facts, as say someone such as Bormann would have been able to.

For now that is where we have to leave it. Sacha Kvap's widow is in Moscow and we will persist in trying to persuade her to elaborate on what we know. In a brief interview on 6 April 1995, she said that her husband always refused to talk about his work during the War. However, among the medals we were shown was one for the "Seizure of Berlin". This is evidence at least, that Kvap was there and made a specific contribution to the fall of the city.

Alexander Kvapishevski – Sasha Kvap – the spy in the Bunker.
This photograph was received by us from Moscow on 12 April 1995

9

HITLER'S SKETCHBOOK

Adolf Hitler, as we have seen, had always seen himself as a *künstler* (artist) and he valued those he considered similarly gifted, such as Albert Speer. We are including this new information about his painting career here because not only were these hitherto unpublished paintings in the sketchbook executed rather later than we had previously thought Hitler had worked, but also they were found in his private suite in the Berlin Bunker: they were obviously of value to him.

In late September 1907, the eighteen-year-old Adolf Hitler arrived in Vienna to sit the examination for entrance to the General School of Painting at the Academy of Fine Arts. Born in 1889 at Braunau on the river Inn, Hitler had been a model pupil at elementary school but had become idle and disrespectful at *Realschule* (secondary school) in Linz and in 1905 had been asked to leave. He had spent the intervening years living with his mother, directionless and over-indulged, living the life of a dandy, going to the opera, sketching and dressing up so as to be taken for a university student with his ivory-topped black cane. He felt he had a talent for drawing, watercolours and architecture; he had even designed a new town hall for Linz, a huge new bridge straddling the river there. With such extravagant ideas it is no surprise that he had high hopes for himself in Vienna.

Hitler was no stranger to Vienna. The year before, he had stayed there with relatives for four weeks, attending the opera and visiting the great museums. He expected the examination at the academy to be "child's play". It was an extraordinary time for the visual arts then, an exciting era in which to be a painter or a sculptor or an architect. In 1897 a small group of artists, dominated by Gustav Klimt, had organised the Vienna Secession, in opposition to the Academy and its conservative exhibition policies. In 1898, the first Secession exhibition was held, showing works by August Rodin, James Whistler and Max Klinger. In 1903, the Secession sponsored the first significant showing

143

in Vienna of paintings by Manet, Degas, Monet, Cézanne, Van Gogh, Renoir and Pissarro. Two years later in Paris, the Fauves had mounted their first show, starring Matisse's *Woman with a Hat*. Also in 1905, Kirchner, Heckel and Schmidt-Rottluff, none of them more than six years older than Hitler, unified in a loose organisation in Dresden to be called *die Brücke* (the Bridge), a name chosen to convey the idea that the work of German artists was by no means cut off from other countries. In 1907, Picasso painted *Les Demoiselles d'Avignon* and, shortly afterwards, met Braque. The first Cubist show took place later that year. In 1909, Emilio Marinetti published his manifesto of futurism and a year after that Guillaume Apollinaire and Max Jacob carried out the first experiments in surrealism. In 1911, the first *Blaue Reiter* exhibition was held in Munich and a year after that Marcel Duchamp completed *Nude Descending a Staircase*. There was a renaissance in painting, with French and German artists playing the major roles.

It was against this explosion of new images, vivid colours, weird and fantastic theories on every side, that the aspiring Adolf Hitler presented himself at the Vienna Academy on the Schillerplatz one morning in early October 1907. He was one of 113 candidates. His father Alois had died in 1903 and his mother Klara was dying. She wanted to see her son settled before she died and agreed he could withdraw the legacy left by his father and move to Vienna to study painting.

The Academy examination was in two parts. The first part covered two three-hour sessions on successive days. It required applicants to execute a number of set pieces, exercises on Christian, mythical or classical themes of which the conservative Academy so heartily approved. One of them was entitled *Excursion* and four drawings by Hitler have survived, landscapes with a surprisingly firm line given the time pressure he was under.

Some thirty-three of the candidates failed this early part of the examination. Hitler succeeded and was admitted to the second stage. Now he had to present his own original "sample drawings" for evaluation by the examiners. He must have hoped that his three years spent sketching in and around Linz would now pay off, that his watercolours of the countryside in Upper Austria would charm the professors.

Of the remaining eighty candidates, a further fifty-two failed the second part. This time Hitler was among them. The Academy records show that his sample drawings were judged "inadequate", and that he had not painted enough heads. Astonished at these insults, he told one companion that the Academy should be blown up.

Much has been made of this failure at the Academy for the effect that it may have had on Hitler's character and the way it shaped his career. Ever afterwards he always hated Vienna and his artistic rejection almost certainly played a part in that feeling.

The world has assumed that Hitler deserved to fail as an artist, that he was not a very good painter and could never have made a living from his brush. However, inadequate attention has been paid to whether the Academy was right to dismiss him. There is certainly evidence that the selectors – as all such selectors – were fallible and, to an extent, unjust. That year, a mere twenty-eight candidates passed both sections of the test. Among those who failed along with Hitler was Robin Christian Andersen, who became a distinguished painter and even held a professorship in the Academy that had once rejected him. Hitler was never as comfortable with the human figure as he was with landscapes and buildings, but in other circumstances he may well have included more figures in his portfolio – one of the reasons given for rejecting him at the second stage. It was as close as that. As Werner Maser was to write in his 1973 biography: "What the world might have been spared if Hitler had included a few more 'heads' in his portfolio can only be conjectured."

After his rejection by the academy, Hitler went to see the Rector, Siegmund l'Allemand. He was told, he said later, that he had little aptitude for painting, that instead his aptitude was for architecture. There is no way of knowing whether l'Allemand meant what he said. He may simply have been fobbing Hitler off with a form of words that was designed to get rid of him. However, after his rejection by the Academy and his talk with l'Allemand, Hitler applied for admission to the architectural school. But here he lacked the formal entry qualifications, one of which was matriculation from regular school, so again he was thwarted from following an artistic career.

At the end of 1907 he returned home, where his mother Klara was now seriously ill. He took charge of the household until she died, shortly before Christmas. There were just the three of them, Klara, his sister Paula and Adolf. He did the washing, the cooking and often supervised Paula's homework (she was eleven in 1907). Despite these personal and professional setbacks, he hadn't given up hope of becoming an artist and a friend of his arranged for an interview with a well-known stage designer, Professor Alfred Roller of the Vienna

Handicrafts School. Roller, it seems, referred Hitler to a certain Panholzer, a Viennese sculptor. Panholzer was an art master at a secondary school and an experienced teacher.

Hitler then presented himself for the Academy the following year, autumn 1908. But this time he failed even the first part of the test. Given the fact that the assessors at the Academy were exactly the same as the year before, they very possibly remembered Hitler and simply dismissed him without giving him the chance to show what he had learned in the meantime. He never even showed them the work he had done for Panholzer.

Still not discouraged, he then set up as an "academic painter" in Vienna to begin with, though he kept himself aloof from recognised artistic circles and stars such as Oskar Kokoschka, Gustav Klimt and Egon Schiele. Throughout 1909 and most of 1910 he painted very many small pictures. At times he produced a picture a day. They were mostly buildings and they were mostly copied from postcards or prints. They were, without exception, lifeless and stilted. But he also executed landscapes and portraits in oil, ink or watercolour and did a number of posters for advertisements – footwear, shoe polish, cosmetics, underwear. During a short stay in a hostel in Meidling, Hitler met Reinhold Hanisch who was a trained draughtsman. Hanisch offered to become his dealer/agent, and managed to sell on many of Hitler's works to both dealers and private individuals. By now Hitler was working mainly in watercolours. They divided the proceeds. The partnership lasted for eight months. Hanisch later wrote (in an undated deposition in the archives of the NSDAP in Coblenz, quoted in Maser), that: "I managed to get quite a lot of custom so that we didn't live too badly."

However, the remark of l'Allemand had struck home and at this stage Hitler was still bent on becoming an architect rather than a painter. So even as business prospered his pictures grew sloppy and superficial. Hanisch urged him to become more thorough and thoughtful but Hitler still had a legacy from his parents – and an allowance as an orphan – and therefore he was not motivated to succeed as Hanisch was. In the summer of 1910 the two men parted.

From the time of his rupture with Hanisch, Hitler delivered his paintings to his clients himself, many of whom at that time were intellectuals or Jews. He also sold via another dealer, a Hungarian Jew called Neumann, who had also lodged in a hostel and so was familiar with the sort of life that Hitler led. His work at this time brought him so much money (in addition to his legacy) that between May 1911 and

April 1913 he voluntarily transferred to one of his sisters, Paula, his orphan's allowance of twenty-five kronen a month.

This was the artistic background that, in large measure, helped form Hitler. He had failed twice before the Academy in Vienna, but he nonetheless did succeed for a while in selling his paintings in sufficient quantities to get by. But his hatred of Vienna grew and he came to believe that he alone knew best about art and that "experts" were not to be trusted. His view became that "real artists" were not the product of traditional academic training but instead needed on-the-job experience with great masters. Above all, he felt that the world had failed to appreciate his gifts.

From Vienna, in May 1913 he moved to Munich, where he continued to sell his paintings. The people he lodged with considered him a "serious artist" because he actually sold his pictures. According to Maser: "He would sit by the window overlooking the school playground on the opposite side of the Schliessheimerstrasse and copy photographs, usually in watercolour but sometimes also in oils. The resulting pictures he sold with some success – mostly to the Kunsthandlung Stuffle in the Maximilianstrasse. His taxable income of 100 marks a month testifies more, perhaps, to his artistic ability than to his business acumen."

According to one of Hitler's biographers, Werner Maser, it has not been possible to ascertain how many pictures he painted over this period of thirteen months though about two dozen "survived the days of the creator's obscurity". This throws into context Ada Petrova's discovery of forty-two paintings in Moscow. This is a sizeable addition to Hitler's *oeuvre*.

After World War One, Hitler's work was sometimes sold by an Army friend, Hans Mend, who filled the role that Hanisch and Neumann had occupied before in Vienna. Hitler always remained ambivalent about his painting. He told Heinrich Hoffmann in 1944 that he produced them only to earn a living, while he pursued his architectural studies. Yet two years earlier, by order of the Ministry of the Interior, his pictures were declared "works of art of national importance" and became subject to registration. One effect of this was that they could not be sold abroad without the written permission of the Ministry.

During the Great War, Hitler produced a number of paintings, among them watercolours executed in France on the front line. *Defile near Wytschaete* and *Ruined Monastery, Messines*, were described by Hermann Nasse, lecturer at the Academy of Fine Arts in Munich: "Here we find the powerful experience of destruction translated into colourful vision. This is not the romanticism of ruins or of war but rather, because of its fluid and painterly treatment, a more grave and moving memorial." But then he *was* writing in 1936 and so was not exactly an objective critic. Heinrich Hoffmann, "Reich photographer to the NSDAP", also thought highly of Hitler's Front Line pictures. "The painting *Dressing Station, Fromelles* belongs to the year 1915. It is rendered in light, sparkling pigment and the buildings with their overhanging eaves are depicted in the most delicate shades and gradations of colour. The watercolour *Haubourdin* of 1916 is truly entrancing. Seen through the eyes of a German painter, the foreign landscape is experienced as something intimate, familiar and animate, indeed even poetic . . . What moves us above all in every one of these pictures is the genuine German sense of dedication, upright, honest and loving, both to the whole and to every minute detail."

After the Armistice, Hitler returned to Munich in the summer of 1919, where he took up certain duties with the Bavarian Army. Despite this, he still harboured hopes of an artistic career of some sort and was hoping to resume his studies, not in architecture but in a regular course of study in art. "For a time he worked with Ernst Schmidt (later mentioned in *Mein Kampf*) with whom he discussed art and architecture. Schmidt-Rottluff, Inkhofer, [Hans] Mend and other army friends owned oil paintings, pastels and drawings in charcoal, pencil and ink made by Hitler during World War One. They were convinced that he possessed artistic talent and urged him to develop it." This all seems to have had an effect on Hitler for he now sought a professional opinion from a well-known local artist named Max Zaeper. Zaeper was impressed, so impressed in fact that he drew Hitler's pictures to the attention of another colleague, Professor Ferdinand Staeger. Staeger was not unknown to Hitler. He had seen Staeger's work at the Vienna Secession exhibition in 1898 and was later to buy several of his pictures. Staeger returned the compliment. His verdict on Hitler's work was: "It shows quite exceptional talent."

Two final points before we come to the new works themselves. The first is that several critics, Franz Jetzinger (author of *Hitler's Youth*) among them, said that Hitler's works were not original but copies, that there was no evidence Hitler ever painted from life. This was not of course true about the paintings he made on the Front during World War One, and it is not true of the paintings we reveal here for the first time. On the contrary, they are packed with detail that can only have been based on close observation.

148

Ivan Paderin, Deputy Commander of a unit of the 8th Guards Army which stormed the Reichschancellery on 2 May 1945. He is being interviewed by Ada Petrova about Sasha Kvap, the spy in the Bunker

Inside the archive where the Operation Myth File is kept. In other hitherto secret archives there are files containing the records of the ss, the Gestapo, the French Security Services and concentration camps such as Auschwitz and Riga

Hitler's Personal Secretary, Martin Bormann, pictured alongside what is alleged to be his skull. It was dug up near the Lehrt Station in Berlin in 1972

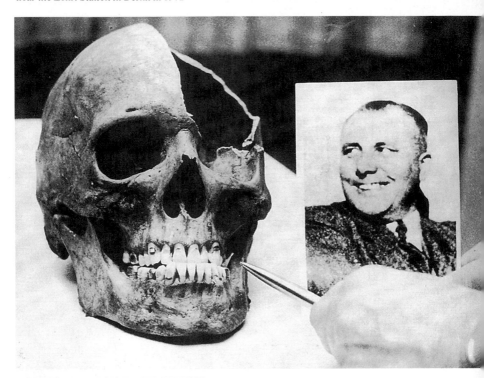

Heinrich Himmler, Head of the Secret Service and once Hitler's heir apparent: *(left)* taking the salute in a march past of Nazi stormtroopers in September 1943. Himmler was denounced by the Führer as a traitor on 29 April 1945 and stripped of all titles

hotographs from Russian interrogation reports held in the Operation Myth File in Moscow: *(above left)* SS
Major-General Wilhelm Mohnke, Commandant of the Reichschancellery; *(above right)* SS General Johann
Rattenhuber, head of Hitler's bodyguards; *(below left)* Heinz Linge, his valet in the Bunker; and *(below right)*
Hans Baur, his personal pilot. Both valet and pilot were released by the Russians in October 1955 at Gottingen
in the East/West German border

Leo Raubal, Hitler's nephew, who was taken prisoner by the Russians near Stalingrad in January 1943. Sentenced to twenty-five years imprisonment, he was actually released in September 1955

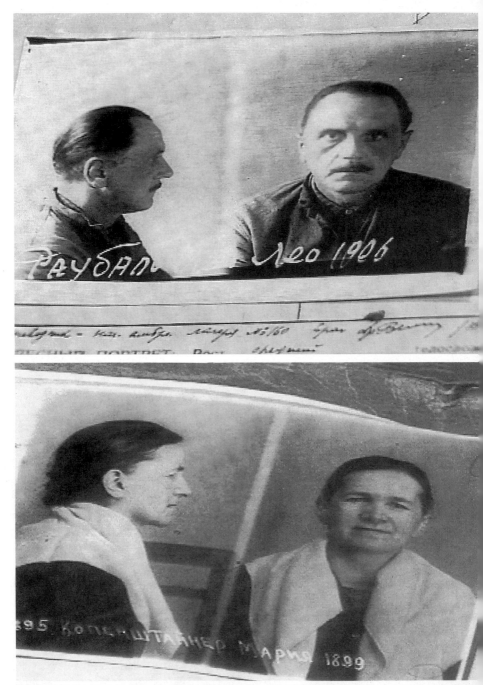

Maria Koppensteiner, the Führer's cousin. She was arrested in May 1945, simply for being related to Hitler. She was treated very badly by the Russians and died "suddenly" in a labour camp in the Upper Urals in 195

Hitler's private photograph gives an indication of how the Führer saw himself.

Here, he is the Bavarian Squire

A friend to animals

With his dog, Blondi

Surrounded by relaxed and happy women

Relaxed in the countryside

Above: The speech-maker in private mood

Left: Taking the wheel of a sailing boat

Right: Hitler was fond of outdoor picnics. Here, with Magda and Josef Goebbels, the mood is mock-serious

Above: Here the mood is festive and good-natured *(from left to right)* Josef Goebbels, Magda Goebbels, Martin Bormann, Adolf Hitler

Right: Adolf Hitler contemplates his mountain retreat, with his long-term mistress and eleventh-hour wife Eva Braun and her sister, Gretl

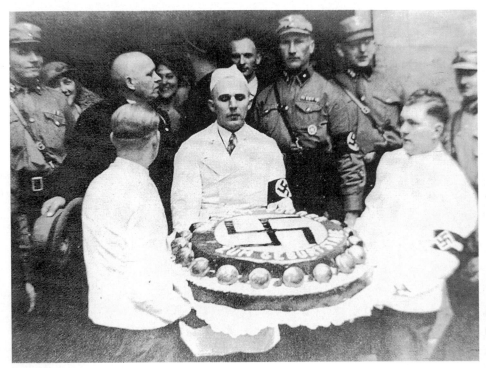

A huge birthday cake baked in honour of Hitler's fifty-fifth birthday, 20 April 1944; and (*below*) a fake collage titled *Jeux de Prince* (the Game of Princes) which was obviously precious enough to be kept in his personal album. While Lord Halifax and Chamberlain lay their cards on the table, Hitler and his partner Mussolini keep their hands to themselves: the Führer has all the aces, the Italian dictator all the court cards. The game is called *Paix* (Peace)

JEUX DE PRINCES

Second, after he became Chancellor, Hitler's attitude to modern art had hardened and in an interesting way. In 1924, according to Ralf Manheim's English translation of *Mein Kampf* published in 1969, he had expressed the view that, by 1900, art had already begun to decline. Gradually, from 1933 onwards the net closed in on all forms of modern art. Most notable was his speech in July 1937 when he opened the exhibition of German art in Munich, across town from the "Degenerate Art" exhibition, which was being shown at the same time. This is when he described modern German artists as: "smearers and blotters, bred by litter rats ... fostered by the Jewry ... prehistoric doodlers [portraying] misformed cripples and cretins, heinous women, men who come nearer to animals than to humans, children who, if they were alive could only be considered a curse of God." At the same time he called for art to be "clear" and "realistic" and ended with a threat to the "pitiful unfortunates" who "attempt to force the results of their deceitful perception upon their contemporaries." Commenting on the blue meadows and green skies of the impressionists and expressionists, he had this to say: "Either these so-called artists see their objects really in this fashion and ... in this case one would have to investigate whether their optical illusion is caused by a mechanical or hereditary deficiency. In the first case, it would be profoundly regrettable for the unfortunates; in the second case it would be of interest to the Ministry of the Interior which would, then, have to take upon itself the task of disrupting the hereditary transmission of such horrible optical disturbances ... Or else these individuals do not themselves believe the reality of their impressions, but impose such humbug on the nation for other reasons. In this case their behaviour becomes the concern of such agencies as are in charge of the enforcement of criminal law."

By 1942 he had developed his views still further. "Up till 1920," he now said – advancing the "deadline" by a couple of decades – "our artistic achievements remained at a remarkably high level. Since then it has unfortunately shown an increasingly rapid decline ... What has been foisted on the German people from 1922 is just one miserable scrawl."

1922. The new date he had chosen was interesting, because it roughly coincided with the point when he himself gave up painting to begin his political career. He was, in effect, placing himself at the end of a nineteenth-century figurative and romantic tradition that turned its back on all the experiments that were happening – impressionism, fauvism, pointillism, cubism – modernism in general. The paintings presented in the colour photo section of this book, therefore take on an added level of interest. For besides not being architectural studies in the main, but landscapes, and besides being the pictures he kept with him until his last days, many of them were produced in the years 1919-21, making them among the last works of Adolf Hitler.

It is worth pointing out, however, that even in regard to Hitler's art, we should bear in mind Ernst-Günther Schenck's strictures and not diabolise Hitler. Just as we show – through our analysis of the pictures themselves – that Hitler was neither a great painter nor a terrible painter, nor was his taste totally philistine or barbaric. In truth, he had a bourgeois taste, he favoured tradition. At the same time, he enjoyed elegance and modern design up to a point. He liked old pictures, good carpets, antique furniture – especially if they made a show – and he could live with modern furnishings. He believed that painting and sculpture had reached their apotheosis in ancient Greece and Rome and that since then only the Baroque and Romantic eras could be called successes. He dismissed Gothic art as too mystical and he thought the Italian renaissance too closely allied to Christianity, and he distrusted all religion.

Where he was contradictory was in his desire to make painting accessible to all. He loathed experts and their jargon but at the same time became himself an expert on the German painters of the nineteenth century that he liked: Eduard Grützner, Wilhelm Liebl, Carl Spitzweg and Hans Thoma. For example, when Heinrich Hoffmann bought some fake Spitzwegs, Hitler spotted them immediately but didn't tell Hoffmann so as to spare the photographer's feelings. Hitler also loved to rediscover "forgotten" artists, which is of course exactly what the experts he loathed were always doing.

What can we say about the new paintings? That there are forty-two of them, that they are small, and were all contained in one *skizzenbuch* (sketchbook). Except for one or two pencil drawings, they are all watercolours.

People, human figures, are notable by their absence – there are maybe three figures only and those are stick people, no more than hinted at. In the more ambitious, finished watercolours, there are no figures whatsoever.

One can also say that there are far fewer buildings than there are landscapes and those buildings there are, are in general far more awkwardly painted than the mountains, trees, fields and fences, lakes and roads. Whereas the mountainsides and meadows are painted with a broad brush, where the colour conveys the *mass*, the buildings are drawn in outline, and not very assured outline at that.

The landscapes all appear to be set in Bavaria. This is lush, mountainous lakeland, with waterfalls, snowcapped peaks, winding roads, meadows bursting with ripe grass.

What stands out here is the sheer assurance with which these pictures are executed. Without going overboard, it is nonetheless true to say that Hitler's sense of composition is first-rate, the perspective is captured accurately, the brushwork gives the paintings a great deal of textural variety and, overall, the mood of the mountains is captured very well.

Looked at closely, the attention to detail is also admirable. In one painting, a view of a meadow, the broken fence is rendered meticulously. In another, of a pine forest, the flowers and twigs on the branches are all painted in the most careful detail. In a third, the colours of the mountainside are varied to match the light, as happens in nature. There is no sense in which these paintings are, in Reinhold Hanisch's dismissal of Hitler's earlier work, "superficial".

Hitler could also create atmospherics. There is among the paintings one of a forest, or pine wood, pictured at the end of the day, with a blazing red sunset beyond. The colours here are very bold, far bolder than many people use in watercolours and far bolder than is usually associated with Hitler. The feeling here is reminiscent of Caspar David, the nineteenth-century German romantic painter.

There is also, dare one say it, an impressionistic quality about some of the paintings. An element of this is inevitable with watercolours, it has to be said. The medium lends itself naturally to light, hesitant brushstrokes, which "suggest" motifs.

The washes of the skies, the broad-brush approach of some of the meadows and the rendering of masses of leaves in the forests, all these have a blurred quality that is part traditional watercolour technique but at the same time is definitely impressionistic. One seascape is atmospheric, not quite in the Turner mode, but getting there.

Another painting is interesting for its iconography. It shows a Bavarian mountain lodge, with hills in the background and a flag on a pole, a black swastika on a red background. Since the swastika was not adopted by the National Socialists until 1919, this proves how late these paintings are. No wonder Hitler never sold them: by then he had other fish to fry.

These watercolours are really interesting. Most of them are very easy on the eye, the works of an accomplished, if not a great, master. Their interest, of course, lies not just in the fact that they have come to light now – and are being presented here for the first time – but that Hitler kept them. As was reported above, he told several people that he painted not because he wanted to be an artist but because he had to live. Yet he didn't sell these. Most of them must have been painted *after* he came back from World War One, when his interests had supposedly shifted from art and architecture to politics.

So did he paint to relax? Is that why they are taken from the life rather than copies? Is that why they are all paintings of landscapes, of Bavaria itself, which was to become the cradle of Naziism? Is that why he kept them? Either way, they strongly suggest that Hitler had – at that stage in his life at any rate – a patience, a concern with detail and a real love of beauty.

These paintings make the transformation of Hitler's character over the following quarter of a century all the more remarkable. Perhaps it is, most of all, a lesson of how every human being is capable of the most contradictory extremes.

10

THE BAVARIAN SQUIRE:
HITLER'S PHOTOGRAPH ALBUM

Just as Hitler kept the forty-two watercolours with him throughout his life and took them to the Bunker, so that they were with him right at the end, so he was also surrounded by about seventy of what appear to have been his favourite photographs. Some of these have been seen before but others, like the watercolours, are new. And, as with the watercolours, they are of interest not just because they are new but also because he kept them. They show the man that Hitler *thought* he was, perhaps the person he wanted to be. As such they cast fresh light on his personality.

Of course, we have to be wary of over-interpreting the album. After all, in most cases the photographs that people keep are the ones that show them in the best light – smiling, in good health, relaxing with friends, winning races not losing them. But even allowing for that, the photographs that Hitler kept in the Bunker show him in a certain light. The picture they build up is consistent and one totally at variance with the Führer we know.

We may follow the discrepancies one by one, to show just how thoroughly misleading the photographs were.

To begin with, for example, many reports of Hitler show him to have been remote and cold, prone to bouts of depression. An analysis of his letters, carried out by Werner Maser, concluded that: "they reveal a singular lack of warmth. They are obviously written by a person who pays heed to others only in so far as they can be of service to him and are prepared to act in accordance with criteria determined by him alone. He seldom asked after his correspondents' health save by way of conventional courtesies, nor did he ever seek their advice. He had no desire to enter into an exchange of ideas and regarded his own opinions as sacrosanct."

In a famous quote, Hermann Rauschning said of Hitler: "Anyone who has met this man face to face, has looked at his uncertain gaze, without depth or warmth, from eyes hard and remote, and has sub-sequently observed that gaze become fixed, will have experienced the strange feeling that the man is strange, not normal." Reinhold Hanisch, the man who sold Hitler's paintings in the early years, said that he also suffered bouts of depression. He said that Hitler just collapsed when there were setbacks or when he was upset. These bouts also went on through World War One when he was in the Army.

And yet the photographs show Hitler as a very warm, cheerful person. He is frequently surrounded by other people, *listening* to them and smiling.

Several reports hinted – and sometimes more than hinted – that Hitler had homosexual tendencies. There are certainly accounts of him being approached by men in search of sexual favours. Most biographers disagree with this diagnosis, but there seems little doubt that, whatever the truth on that score, he had a low opinion of women. He was regarded as a "lady-killer" in Munich, had a number of affairs. Later, after he became a prominent political figure, all manner of women were infatuated with him and his power, to such an extent that rich admirers became important early benefactors of the Nazi Party, offering not just money but *objets d'art* as well.

But this was all for public consumption and an act. Speaking in private when no women were present, Hitler was a misogynist and would talk contemptuously and slightingly of marriage and the female sex in general. On 25-26 January 1942, according to Henry Pickers in his book on Hitler's conversations, the Führer declared: "The worst of marriage is that it creates demands. That's why it is far better to keep a mistress." He further qualified this statement by saying that "only outstanding men" should do so. "A man should be able to leave his stamp on a girl. It's what women like." A few weeks later, he had this to say: "When a woman starts thinking about the problems of existence that's bad ... apt to get on one's nerves." This was clearly a matter on his mind at the time for in March 1942 he returned to the subject: "A man's world is big compared with a woman's ... The man is all her world. Only occasionally does she think of anything else ... A woman's love is deeper than a man's. Her intellect is of no great consequence."

His behaviour, as time went by, reinforced his views. Especially during the War, his private encounters with women became fewer and fewer. The only women he saw regularly were his personal secretaries and his cook. Not even his mistress of twelve-year's standing, Eva Braun, was allowed into his headquarters at Wolfsschanze in East Prussia.

You would never guess any of this from the photographs. A good many of them show Hitler in the company of – seemingly at ease with – several women. There are picnics, walks in the mountains, formal occasions in the evening when he has a woman on each arm. The gatherings are intimate, warm, jolly, everyone is relaxed and smiling. Sometimes the women are listening to him, sometimes he seems engrossed in what they have to say.

Hitler was an introvert. So say his biographers, who add that by and large he was "incapable of deep attachments". All his early friends, if they can be called that, were cast aside as soon as it suited him. After 1937 he became even more aloof. By then he believed himself to be seriously ill and "ceased to have any close rapport with the men who had worked with him and fought at his side." Part of the same coin was his inability to engage in small talk. Albert Speer was only one of many to pick up on this. It was, he told Hugh Thomas, "*the* feature that made most [of Hitler's] acquaintances uneasy."

By the same token, Hitler could not tolerate criticism and would leave meetings where his viewpoint was challenged. Otto Strasser, one of his rivals in the Nazi Party in the early days (and therefore not entirely reliable as an objective witness), said that Hitler was very uncomfortable when he was not the acknowledged expert on whatever subject was under discussion. This was paradoxical, of course, for a man who loathed expertise in others. But the point here is that the photographs don't bear this out. In one, Hitler is on the telephone, utterly engrossed in what the person at the other end has to say. These are not affairs of state being discussed, we are asked to believe, but instead a juicy piece of malicious gossip. You cannot imagine the Hitler of these photographs ever storming out of a meeting because someone didn't agree with him.

From 1937 onwards, Hitler "avoided all physical exertion." He gave up skiing and by 1940 was convinced that he was terminally ill. He had a check-up which lasted for several days in January that year. He was found to have a high blood pressure and intermittent stomach and digestive disorders (including flatulence), but otherwise was in good health.

It made no difference. He continued to believe that he was very ill and would even leaf through professional medical journals on the off-chance that he would find what was wrong with him. Later that year he underwent another examination, after which his behaviour began to deteriorate, when his blood pressure remained high. He became more peremptory, even aggressive. This may have owed something to the drugs that Dr Morell was prescribing, especially Pervitin which is a stimulant.

The photographs do not show Hitler as an athlete, exactly, but they do not show him as an invalid either. There is a photo of him on a sled, at the wheel of a boat on a lake, out walking with his dog Blondi, he is calm, reflective, quietly reading the paper, dressed in plus fours, ready for a tramp across the mountainside. A million miles from the rallies in the big cities, the Hitler of the photographs is a country squire without a care in the world.

In his study of Hitler's intellectual background, Werner Maser examined Hitler's reading and his knowledge levels. He concluded that Hitler regarded History (with a capital H) as the work of great men. The Führer downplayed sociological thought – especially that of Marx – but he was impressed by biological theories, such as those Jacob Burckhardt, who regarded nations as biological organisms subject to natural laws. Hitler was particularly taken with the ideas of Thomas Robert Malthus, the late eighteenth-century English economist and clergyman, who was the first to warn against the dangers of overpopulation: unlike Malthus, Hitler regarded overpopulation as desirable, as a means to an end which it would compel a fit nation (but only a fit nation) to "bestir itself", wage war on its enemies and create extra room which the fit peoples would occupy at the expense of the unfit.

As part of this, war became an important part of Hitler's thinking. Maser quotes a paper given to the Eighth Conference of the International Planned Parenthood Federation, meeting in Chile in 1967, when the Scottish psychiatrist, Professor Carstairs, of Edinburgh University, quoted results of experiments which showed that certain species of animals show disorganisation of their normal behaviour when confined to pens which had been deliberately overcrowded. Maser continued: "Hitler's markedly emotional reactions when dealing with the problem of war and territorial expansion bear a close parallel to those of the animals described by Carstairs. Whenever he broached the subject of *Volk und Raum* (people and space) in relation to war, he would for a time become alarmingly and distressingly vehement, so that the impression he gave was of a fanatically committed psychopath acting instinctively in a state of bellicose exaltation. The blood rushed almost visibly to his head, his features became congested, his body rigid, he threw out his chest and thrust forward his arm as though to seize or strike down an adversary ... to what extent his behaviour was due to high blood pressure and the effects of constant medication is not readily ascertainable."

The Hitler in the photograph album is not a war-monger. One might have expected Hitler to be proud of his skills as an orator, his ability to move people, to stir them to a frenzy. This power was unrivalled, set him apart from lesser individuals, was indeed one of the main planks on which he built the Third Reich. The rallies and the parades were an important part of the propaganda that helped make the Reich what it was. It will be remembered the testimonies of his valet Linge and his SS Adjutant Günsche, that Hitler was a sentimentalist. After he made an important speech, he would return to his hotel or apartment, take a shower, then relax with a shot of vodka in a cup of hot tea. On these occasions, his dinner guests were allowed *only* to reminisce about the early days of National Socialism, its great early victories when they had "thrashed" communism. It is this sentimentalism that is hinted at in the photographs he surrounded himself with in the last days.

In February 1944 Hitler's health began to deteriorate yet further. He complained of a sudden change in the condition of his right eye, both in terms of clarity of vision and because he had a stabbing pain behind the eyeball. A vitreous haemorrhage was diagnosed. More drugs were prescribed and a specialist, Walter Löhlein, also recommended that the Führer be spared undue excitement – hardly practical at the time of Monte Cassino and the run-up to D Day.

This illness altered Hitler's behaviour. He needed to use a magnifying glass to read but, more profoundly, he became more outrageous, more distrustful, more hysterical. He had also developed a pronounced stoop.

After the attempt on his life in July 1944, existence became even more of a torment. He was under constant physical and mental strain, his body was flooded with drugs, the military news was almost all bad, he was required to live underground for much of the time, his vegetarian diet was unvaried and he could sleep for but three or four hours a night, sometimes not even that.

In October 1944 he took another turn for the worse. On the first of the month he was examined by Dr Giesing, who found that Hitler's pulse was rapid and faint. In fact, the Führer actually lost consciousness for a little while on that day. His doctors fell out about his treatment, some of them believing that the antigas pills that Morell was prescribing were actually dangerous.

A related factor was Hitler's uncleanliness and his terrible body odour. Speer has spoken vividly about how he dreaded Hitler shedding his coat in summer and working in his shirtsleeves. The stench, Speer said, was overwhelming.

This, combined with Hitler's uncontrollable flatulence, the state of his living quarters – especially in the last days – and the foodstains on his clothes, especially in the later days, hardly presents an attractive picture.

Not surprisingly, the photographs which have survived seem to go out of their way to paint Hitler as a very natty dresser, almost, one might say, as a dandy. Whereas in public he was invariably seen in uniform, his uniform in these photographs is notable by its rarity. The Führer is shown in white tie and tails, in tweeds, in Austrian shorts. These clothes are always neat and tidy, and fit him well. He wears them a trifle self-consciously, but that may be because he realises they are the height of fashion, at least for a Bavarian squire. The man in these photographs has no body odour, no flatulence, no drug problems. One even shows him with a bird on his shoulder. He could almost be a model for the Bavarian good life in a mail-order catalogue.

Regarding Hitler's personal relationships with his close entourage, two things stand out from these photographs. One is that Eva Braun hardly gets any special treatment. She had made her play for Hitler in September 1931, after Geli Raubal – his mistress and daughter of his half-sister Angela – had committed suicide and he was in deep despair. Eva had moved in with him in early 1932. After that she was never far away, though there were times when she became very jealous. (In November 1932 she attempted to commit suicide herself by shooting herself in the throat. She made another attempt, by poisoning, in May 1935.)

An indicator of the relationship between Hitler and Eva was that even when writing to her sister, she referred to him as "the Führer". She remained out of the limelight, as he wished, and in her diary wrote: "He needs me only for certain purposes ... it can't be otherwise ... When he says he loves me, he only means it at that moment." She pressed Morrell, according to Morrell, to give Hitler drugs to stimulate his sexual desire. Aware of his liking for big-bosomed women, she apparently used to stuff handkerchiefs into her brassière.

Given all this, it is perhaps only natural that Eva should not be singled out in the photographs.

The same cannot be said about Goebbels. It is fair to say that the

Propaganda Minister occupied a special place in Hitler's scheme of things. Hitler, after all a master orator, whose real genius lay as much in propaganda as in anything else, needed another genius as his Propaganda Minister while he himself was fulfilling other functions. Goebbels truly understood Hitler's genius but was aware of his own, too. In 1935 he said: "What would have become of this movement without propaganda? And what would have become of this state were it not for the truly creative propaganda which still today provides it with an intellectual face?" Goebbels, with Speer, was the only senior minister by whom Hitler, at the end, did not feel betrayed or disappointed with.

But, unlike Speer, Goebbels and his entire family were on intimate terms with the Führer. Goebbels it was who used to read to Hitler in the early evenings from the one-volume German edition of Thomas Carlyle's *Life of Frederick the Great.* Count Luz Schwerin von Krosigk, Hitler's Finance Minister, quoted Goebbels as telling him about a lifetime horoscope for Hitler drawn up on 30 January 1933, the day he became Chancellor. This had forecast: "The outbreak of world war in 1939, amazing victories until 1941, a series of setbacks in the early months of 1945, to be followed by an overwhelming victory in the second half of April 1945 . . ." When Magda and Josef had wanted to separate in 1938, Hitler had intervened – partly because Goebbels' new love was a Czech, a member of a despised Slav race. Even though Magda was a divorced woman with "a past", the Goebbels family were supposed to be the living embodiment of the Nazi aryan ideal. In 1941 Hitler confided his worries about his heart condition to very few people, but among them Goebbels.

And, of course, it was the Goebbels family whom Hitler asked to join him in the Bunker in the last days. It was Goebbels who was one of the witnesses to his marriage with Eva; it was Goebbels who witnessed Hitler's Will and Political Testament; it was Goebbels who, for a time, talked Hitler out of immediate suicide on 22 April. He was ever the propagandist, ever the disciple.

Goebbels used Hitler's frenzied glare in many carefully stage propaganda photographs. These were responsible for the idea that Hitler was a ferocious monster, brilliant and evil, cunning and strong, all-seeing and invincible.

None of these photographs was kept in the Bunker, but such photographs as do survive show that Goebbels was the only senior officer who Hitler admitted frequently to his close circle. Goebbels is at all the picnics. If Hitler was close to one man, especially in the later years, if any man could be regarded as a friend, a soulmate, then Goebbels fulfilled that role for Hitler, at least as shown by the photographs. He was closer to Hitler than he was to Eva Braun.

So the Hitler in the photograph album is Onkel Adolf, a paternalistic, cheerful, dapper, friendly individual, who enjoyed the company of a select group of individuals. As revealed by these photographs, Hitler had an image of himself that was totally at variance with reality. It was as if he had some conception of a golden age, of picnics, boat rides, walks in the woods, intimate gatherings, where he was just one among a number of stylish friends without a care in the world, where the sun shone and it was always summer. Where men were at ease with women and with each other.

It is perhaps incomprehensible to us that a man whose fanatical politics had sent millions of Jews, Poles and others to their deaths could see himself in this light. Did he really believe he was an *ordinary* individual who did not stand out in any way in domestic situations?

Perhaps what these photos really show is that Adolf Hitler was – over and above the normal reaches of human response – a man capable of being seduced by his own propaganda.

That is not unimportant. Hitler's photographic album may be a warning – if a warning were needed – that the sentimentalist with power is the most dangerous type of all.

EPILOGUE: OTHER SECRETS IN
THE RUSSIAN ARCHIVES

The fascination with Hitler has lasted for fifty years. So has the obsession with the manner of his death. This need not have happened but for the Soviet Union's irresponsible behaviour regarding the release of documents and other materials relating to its investigations in the aftermath of the War. The Russians' explanation for keeping this material hidden, unpublished in its entirety, is that they wanted to keep something "in reserve", in case pretenders should claim that Hitler had, after all, escaped by some miracle. That is almost certainly only half the reason. Stalin obviously had his own agenda and, as Sergei Kondrashov told us, he was an unpredictable man. Stalin's full reasons for telling lies about the corpse of Hitler may never be known.

Added to that, there does seem to have been a series of errors on the Russian side which led to a cover-up. The first commission undoubtedly botched the investigation, failing to test the internal organs for cyanide poisoning. This was probably more to do with circumstance than design: it was VE day and the doctors wanted to be part of the celebrations, so they cut short the autopsy. Prosaic, but all too human.

At any event, doubts about the first commission grew. Was this also because the Soviets doubted their own experts given how convinced the West was that Hitler had shot himself? Or was it, again, Stalin, who wanted to be doubly sure that his old adversary was truly dead? Either or both could explain the setting up of a second commission.

The second commission naturally complicated matters, especially when blood was found on the walls of Hitler's living room in the Bunker and the skull with the bullet hole turned up in the very crater where the Führer's body had been found. This revealed the first commission as having been seriously incompetent and, in Stalinist Russia, that was a major crime. Smersh had blundered in the most important of cases. Surely this explains why they then refused to make available

161

the Hitler and Braun corpses? It may even explain why they buried them so thoroughly, entombed beneath asphalt at their own headquarters. Smersh was protecting its own. This battle – between Smersh and its rivals for the custody of Hitler's remains – is a story that also should be told. It would be a narrative worthy of John le Carré.

The publication of Lev Bezymenski's book looks just as strange now as ever. Why publish – or allow to be published – a story that is incomplete and wrong? Was it part of some sophisticated attempt at disinformation on the part of the Soviets or was it rather that one part of the security services wanted their side told, knowing that if they did it would always be difficult for the Russians to go back on that first official version without losing face? The documents we have seen unfortunately throw no light on this.

We showed, at the very beginning of this book, that the Allies had allowed themselves to be misled about the Alpine Redoubt, catastrophically so in some ways. Hitler had planned to go south, to try to run the remainder of the war from the OberSalzberg, but there was never any real possibility of a prolonged resistance run from the mountains. The specialist Werewolf troops created specially for the purpose were no more than figments of the imagination.

Similarly, despite colourful accounts of such organisations as ODESSA, the Bormann Brotherhood and *die Spinne* – not to mention constant "sightings" of Bormann *et al* – the worries that there would ever be a resurgent Nazi movement even remotely resembling that which came to power in 1933 have proved illusory. Just as the Alpine Redoubt was a myth, so was the Fourth Reich a non-starter in all but the warped minds of a few.

Thus there really is no justification for the obsessive secrecy with which the Russians have treated the material presented here over the past fifty years. Even now it has been dragged into the open by a journalist after a chance comment, rather than an official source.

One final point on the Bunker. The very fact that the Russians *did* institute two commissions on the death of Hitler, secret commissions, surely proves that they did not know everything that was going on inside that concrete monstrosity. Bormann could not have been their spy.

The death of Hitler has been one of the great detective stories of the second half of the twentieth century. Perhaps, the greatest. Many people have spent years patiently piecing together the many details of this complicated picture. The skull and documents known as the Operation Myth File surely provide the last word on the matter, with perhaps one exception.

We make this plea. It is known where certain relatives of Hitler are living. With the DNA fingerprinting techniques now available, it is possible to test both these individuals and the organic materials in Moscow (the jaw and skull bones) to examine whether they all share vital genetic material. Such scientific analysis could resolve this matter, one way or the other, beyond all reasonable doubt. The fiftieth anniversary of the end of the War is surely an appropriate time to make such a test so that we may all put this contentious issue behind us.

There is a related matter, too, which ought not to go unmentioned. Many more documents pertaining to unresolved details about World War Two are known to be in the secret archives of the former Soviet Union. We can reveal that these archives contain the records of the SS, the Gestapo, the French security services and a thousand files of the British Army that were lost to the Germans during the Dunkirk retreat and then confiscated by the Russians at the end of the War. The same applies to the British Army's records of Tobruk, two years after Dunkirk. For the French, the files in Russia expose the links between that country's security services and the Vichy government, potentially a very embarrassing matter. There is Polish, Czech and even Italian material which is illuminating and no less embarrassing (anti-partisan activity in northern Italy, for example). There are SS and SD files on Auschwitz and Riga, which could settle some important questions once and for all. There are files on Hermann Rauschning, Thomas Mann and Walter Rathenau, on Hjalmar Schacht and Goebbels himself. There is a file on the Reichschancellery.

The amount of material is copious. We look forward to a time when these documents are shared openly. World War Two was almost certainly the most atrocious set of events in world history. Details about the art works which were taken from Germany have already been made public and now we are presenting the evidence on Hitler's remains. But there is much more that could be revealed. The Russians owe it to humanity to see that the full – and unexpurgated – history of those tragic years can at last be written.

Appendix A:

THE FATE OF HITLER'S RELATIVES

The documents we have seen describe the arrest and post-War fate of two of Hitler's blood relatives. The first of these is Maria Koppensteiner, his cousin. Born in 1899, her mother was Teresia Pölzl, sister to Klara, Hitler's mother.

In the biographies of Hitler that we have consulted, there is no record of Maria, But the Russian archives tell us that she married an Ignaz Koppensteiner, a miller from the village of Langfeld, near Waitra, which is 160 kilometres from Vienna. They had four children, the last of whom was born in 1940, a boy called Adolf.

Maria was arrested by Smersh agents at the end of May 1945, as were three of her brothers. (There is no record of these, either, in the Hitler biographies we have consulted). A fourth brother was arrested by the British.

She was taken to Lefortovo prison in Moscow and interrogated many times. The files say that she gave this testimony: "Only after hundreds of such interrogations when she was psychologically broken and finally understood what the interrogators wanted to get from her."

Maria Koppensteiner said that she was very friendly with Paula, Hitler's sister, who had often sent clothes for her children. When her mother (Hitler's aunt) died, he sent money for the funeral. While Paula was herself being supported by her brother, she would pass on anything between 100 and 200 marks to Maria. In 1938, she and her brother Anton had planned to travel to Nuremberg for a holiday and to visit their relative, the Führer. However, Paula dissuaded them from going, saying that Hitler did not like having his family around at close quarters.

The strange wording of the testimony – in which Maria didn't break until she realised what the interrogators wanted – appears to be a reference to the confession she eventually made. It branded her cousin as a War criminal, waging "aggressive" war, "occupying" countries, "plundering", "ruining" cities and "destroying" civilisations, turning people into slaves. It would seem at that stage that the Soviet authorities were contemplating using these statements of Maria Koppensteiner's for some sort of propaganda purposes, perhaps to counter the claims of any "Hitler" who might resurface in the wake of the War.

However, her testimony was never needed. After her trial – no details of this are given – she was sentenced to twenty-five years in prison. She was eventually transferred to one of the worst of the Soviet camps, the Upper Urals prison near Chelyabinsk. According to one document she died there "suddenly" in 1953. There are, however, strong grounds for believing that she was killed, possibly by lethal injection. What her crimes were – other than being a relative of Hitler's – is never explained in the documents.

The second relative of Hitler who is mentioned in the documents is Leo Raubal. Born in Linz in 1906, Leo Raubal was the son of Angela Hitler, Adolf's half-sister and therefore a brother to Angela Raubal – Geli – with whom Hitler was desperately in love in the 1920s. (As an artist, he once claimed the right to draw Geli in the nude, producing by all accounts some obscene sketches which were later stolen and had to be bought back from a blackmailer.) Geli lived in Hitler's apartment on Prinzregentenplatz in Munich.

She was the first – and perhaps the only – woman that Hitler had loved and he flew into jealous rages if she did not follow his wishes slavishly. It was after one of their arguments, on 18 September 1931, that she shot herself through the heart with one of Hitler's own Walther 6.35 revolvers. There were all sorts of rumours about her death, the most damaging of which was that Hitler had had her killed, by Himmler, because she had become pregnant by a Jewish boyfriend. In fact, Hitler's infatuation and his vicious rages had driven her to suicide. He was inconsolable and remained in solitary seclusion for two weeks, during which time he was apparently close to suicide himself.

For the remainder of his life Hitler observed a cult in honour of the woman he had driven to death. "It was a strange cult without ceremonies or rites; he demanded of her only that she be present at all times. He carried her photograph wherever he travelled, just as he carried the photograph of his mother. The room in the Prinzregentenplatz where [Geli] killed herself was kept exactly as she left it, and only Hitler and Annie Winter, who brought flowers every day, were permitted to enter it. An obscure second-rate painter named

Adolf Ziegler was commissioned to paint her portrait from a photograph, and this painting, nearly full length, occupied a place of honour in the reception room at OberSalzberg, and there was always a bowl of fresh flowers beneath it," so it is quoted in Robert Payne's biography of Hitler.

Leo Raubal was taken prisoner near Stalingrad on 31 January 1943. His file (number 03-1878564) is preserved in the Archive of the Ministry of Internal Affairs, Chief Directorate of POWs and Internees. A member of the NSDAP since 1922, he had graduated from the school for Reserve officers. He was a businessman throughout the 1930s but, as a Reserve officer, was called up to the Air Force on 2 October 1939, less than a month after War broke out. He became Adjutant to the Commander of his regiment, with the rank of Lieutenant. He was awarded the Iron Cross, second class.

He was kept in prison camps 160, 190 and 185. An extract from the prison sentence passed on him on 27 December 1949, reads as follows: "Defendant Raubal, being a relative of the main War criminal, Hitler, supported his aggressive policy, took part in the sessions of the Reichstag and in the atrocities perpetrated on the territory of Ukraine, Orel, Smolensk, Bobruisk regions and in Stalingrad." He was found guilty of crimes committed on the territory of the Soviet Union and sentenced to twenty-five years. (Raubal would undoubtedly have been executed but for the fact that, since 1942, capital punishment had officially been abolished in Soviet Russia.)

Raubal was put in the "punishment cell" several times, accused of "sabotage". His appeals against this treatment were rejected. In the file there is a letter from his wife Anne, a Frenchwoman, asking for him to be pardoned because she and her two children were "in severe need and don't have any means of subsistence." This too was rejected.

He was finally released on 28 September 1955.

Few conclusions can be drawn from such meagre evidence, other than to say that the Russians appear to have done their homework well in advance regarding Hitler's immediate – and not so immediate – family. As a fighting soldier, Leo Raubal appears to have been treated no better and no worse than anyone else. But Maria Koppensteiner *was* treated badly. There is no evidence that she was anything other than an ordinary German citizen, not a War criminal. To the Russians, however, no blood-relative of Hitler could ever be "ordinary".

Appendix B:

RUSSIAN ARCHIVES CONSULTED DURING
RESEARCH

The material for this book was researched in ten archives in Russia. As an aid to others investigating this topic, this is a brief resumé of what was found where.

1. **Archive of the Ministry of Internal Affairs**
   Prison files; inmates registration forms; records of interrogations; some data on inmates' fate after the sentence.

2. **Archive of the Federal Counter-Intelligence Service (former KGB Archive)**
   The jaw; Hitler and Eva Braun's personal belongings; records of the first interrogations of Hitler's closest entourage conducted in Germany; report of the first commission; Rattenhuber's memoirs; Günsche's testimony and documents pertaining to the destruction of the remains of Hitler and Braun in 1970.

3. **Archive of the Museum of the Armed Forces**
   Hitler's uniforms; Swastika armbands; the "Conqueror of Europe" rug; the gifts donated on the anniversary of his fiftieth birthday.

4. **Archive of the External Intelligence and former Archive of the Central Committee of the Communist Party of the Soviet Union**
   Various documents and correspondence pertaining to the two commissions. Used to corroborate material elsewhere.

5. **State Archive of the Russian Federation**
   The skull; fragments of the blood-stained sofa; six volumes of interrogation records of Hitler's entourage.

6. **Archive of the President of the Russian Federation**
   The originals of many of the internal memoranda, reports and correspondence. (This was important, in the wake of the Hitler diaries fiasco, as a safeguard against forgery.)

7. **Centre for Storage of Historical and Documentary Collections (former State Special Trophy Archive)**
   Hitler's book of honorary guests; his autographs; the watercolours; prison files and photographs.

8. **Krasnogorsk Archive of Film and Photographic Documents**
   Film documentaries, from which the photographs of Beria and Stalin and the Goebbels family, were taken.

9. **Defence Ministry Archive**
   Documents about World War Two and the Battle of Berlin, for cross-checking the sequence of events.

10. **Special Section of the Russian State Library (former Lenin Library)**
    The photograph album, plus photographs of the Reichschancellery during the last days.

ANNOTATED BIBLIOGRAPHY

Bernadotte, Count Folke, *The Curtain Falls*, New York, Alfred A. Knopf, 1945.
Eyewitness account of the fall of Berlin, plus pen-picture of Himmler during his attempt to surrender in the west.

Bezymenski, Lev, *The Death of Adolf Hitler: Unknown Documents from Soviet Archives*, London, Michael Joseph, 1968.
Son of a poet, Bezymenski served in the armed forces at Stalingrad, where he acted as interpreter at the hearings of General Paulus, the German Field-Marshal who surrendered to the Russians after the battle, and on Marshal Zhukov's staff in Berlin. This is the book that describes the work of the first Russian commission. For some reason Bezymenski was not given access to any details about the second commission and only very incomplete information about the interrogations of Linge, Günsche *et al.* This, of course, is the basis for Chapter 3 of this book and forms part of the discussions in Chapters 6 and 7.

Byford-Jones, W, *Berlin Twilight*, London, Hutchinson, 1963.
A little known book but the author was in Berlin in the summer of 1945, did visit the Bunker and made a number of astute observations. Chapter 2, "Inquest on Hitler", contains an eyewitness report of the press conference at which Trevor-Roper released his preliminary findings.

Casey, William, *The Secret War Against Hitler*, London, Simon & Schuster, 1989.
Later in life, Bill Casey was Director of the CIA under President Reagan. This book is a history of the Allied – and especially American – Intelligence in World War Two. He examines the National Redoubt

myth and finds that the "Pickaxe" teams dropped into Bavaria concluded that the Redoubt was *not* a serious concept. But these men on the ground were not listened to. This book was used for the material in Chapter 1.

Dietrich, Otto, *The Hitler I Knew*, London, Methuen K, 1957.

Eisenhower, General Dwight, *Crusade in Europe*, New York, Doubleday, 1948.

Irving, David (editor), *Adolf Hitler: The Medical Diaries: The Private Diaries of Dr Theo Morell*, London, Sidgwick & Jackson, 1983.
A detailed analysis of Hitler's medical condition from 1941 to the end, closely related to the events of the War. Hitler's physical deterioration was never more in evidence. There is a final chapter on the behaviour of Dr Morrell in captivity.

Leahy, William D, *I Was There*, London, Gollancz, 1950.

Maser, Werner, *Hitler, Legend, Myth and Reality*, London, Harper & Row, 1973.
A very full, thorough, stolid biography, one of the first to examine Hitler's ailing health as an explanation for some of the decisions he took, especially in the later years of the War. This book was used throughout for verification of facts about Hitler, but especially in Chapters 8, 9 and 10.

Galante, Pierre (with Eugène Silianoff), *Last Witnesses in the Bunker*, London, Sidgwick & Jackson, 1989.
This book is basically the story of Frau Trudl Junge, one of Hitler's secretaries. The book makes Hitler out to have been much more human than other accounts, portraying his love of animals, his civility to women and so on. It may usefully be read alongside Chapter 10 of this book.

Galante, Pierre (with Eugène Silianoff), *Operation Valkyrie: The German Generals' Plot Against Hitler*, New York, Harper & Row, 1981.
Useful information on General Schmundt. Used in Chapter 8.

O'Donnell, James, *The Berlin Bunker*, London, J.M. Dent & Sons, 1979.
O'Donnell was in Berlin in 1945 as a soldier. Later, as a journalist for *Newsweek* based in Berlin, he never lost his interest in the final days of the War and, in the 1960s and 1970s with the help of Rochus Misch, he tracked down many of the survivors, uncovering much new material. This is the book on which Chapter 4 is based.

Payne, Robert, *The Life and Death of Adolf Hitler*, London, Jonathan Cape, 1979.
Used throughout, but especially thorough on Hitler's early years and Leo Raubal, discussed in Appendix A.

Pogue, Forrest C, "The Decision to Halt on the Elbe, 1945" in *Command Decisions*, Kent Greenfield (editor), London, Methuen, 1960.
Background on the Allied military thinking in the final months of the War.

Ryan, Cornelius, *The Last Battle*, London, Collins, 1966.
A gripping account of the Battle of Berlin by the author of *The Longest Day* and *A Bridge Too Far*. Meticulously researched, the last chapter places the events in the Bunker in their wider context. Ryan researched his book in Russia and East Germany at a time when such research was a good deal more difficult than it is now. Used for Chapters 1, 4, 7, 8 and 10.

Sayer, Ian, and **Botting, Douglas,** *America's Secret Army: The Untold Story of the Counter Intelligence Corps*, London, Grafton, 1989.
Two chapters, "Overruning the Reich" and "In the Ruins of the Reich", examine the Redoubt myth and the Allies' search for Hitler in the summer and autumn of 1945. Used for Chapter 1.

Sherwood, Robert E, *The White House Papers of Harry L. Hopkins* (two vols), London, Eyre & Spottiswode, 1948.

Stevenson, William, *The Bormann Brotherhood*, London, Arthur Barker, 1973.
A rambling book but with nuggets of solid gold scattered throughout. Tantalising glimpses of the spy in the Bunker, Sightings of Bormann, what the Russians had on the death of Hitler, *die Spinne* and ODESSA.

Thomas, Hugh, *Doppelgänger: The Truth about the Bodies in the Berlin Bunker,* London, Fourth Estate, 1995.

The author is a doctor, an international authority on gunshot wounds. In *The Murder of Rudolf Hess,* 1979, he created a furore by suggesting that the prisoner of Spandau was not Hess. In *Doppelgängers,* he argues that the bodies found in the crater in the Reichschancellery garden did not belong to either Adolf Hitler or Eva Braun. These arguments are refuted in Chapters 5, 6 and 7 of this book.

Toland, John, *Adolf Hitler,* New York, Doubleday, 1976.

Thorough, especially useful for details on General Schmundt. Used in Chapter 8.

Trevor-Roper, Hugh, *The Last Days of Hitler,* New York, Macmillan, 1947.

This celebrated classic has now, by 1995, been into seven editions. A substantial introduction was added for the 1956 edition, to take into account the stories by Linge, Baur and others following their release from Russia in 1955. Trevor-Roper did not fully address the findings of Bezymenski, leaving himself open to criticism from other authors such as Hugh Thomas.

Warlimont, Walter, *Inside Hitler's Headquarters, 1939-45,* New York, Praeger, London, Weidenfeld & Nicolson, 1964.

Especially useful for Schmundt and used in Chapter 8.

Werth, Alexander, *Russia: The Post-War Years,* London, Robert Hale, 1971.

Chapter 2, "The Difficult Summer of 1945", examines the behaviour of Stalin, Zhukov and Chuikov against a background of the Soviet agenda in the developing Cold War. Helpful in understanding (although not excusing) why the Russians behaved as they did.

INDEX